TOWARDS A ZERO-COST ECONOMY

A BLUEPRINT TO CREATE GENERAL ECONOMIC SECURITY IN A CAREFREE ECONOMY

Farid A. Khavari, PhD

iUniverse, Inc.
New York   Bloomington

Towards A Zero-Cost Economy
A Blueprint to Create General Economic Security in a Carefree Economy

iUniverse books may be ordered through booksellers or by contacting:

iUniverse
1663 Liberty Drive
Bloomington, IN 47403
www.iuniverse.com
1-800-Authors (1-800-288-4677)

Because of the dynamic nature of the Internet, any Web addresses or links contained in this book may have changed since publication and may no longer be valid. The views expressed in this work are solely those of the author and do not necessarily reflect the views of the publisher, and the publisher hereby disclaims any responsibility for them.

ISBN: 978-1-4401-2168-5 (pbk)
ISBN: 978-1-4401-2169-2 (ebk)

Printed in the United States of America

iUniverse rev. date: 2/19/2009

DEDICATION

This book is dedicated to all Americans. I hope the implementation of its concepts will make the American Dream a reality for everybody.

Also by Farid A. Khavari

- **Carefreeism** – Economic Security in a Carefree Economy (in preparation)
- **The Final Reckoning** – The Islamic Plot to Destroy the Dollar, U.S.A., 1995
- **Environomics** – The Economics of Environmentally Safe Prosperity, U.S.A.,1993
- **Oil & Islam** – The Ticking Bomb, U.S.A.,1990
- **Vultures** – Doctors, Lawyers, Hospitals and Insurance Companies, U.S.A, 1990
- **Die OPEC im weltwirtschaftlichen Spannungsfeld** – Ein Beitrag zur Discussion um die "neue Weltwirtschaftsordnung", (OPEC and the New World Economic Order), Germany, 1996
- **Die Oelpreispolitik der OPEC-Laender** – Grenzen, Gruende und Hintergruende (The Oil Price Policy of the OPEC Countries - Limits, Reasons and Backgrounds) Germany, 1995
- **Die Oelkrisen bedrohen den Wohlstand des Westens**, (The Oil Crises Threatening the Prosperity of the West, Germany, 1973
- **Sepahe danesh dar rahe sazendegiye roustaha**, (Education Corp in Building the Villages), Iran, 1964

Table of Contents

IMPORTANT NOTES AND ANNOUNCEMENT

The blueprint you are about to read is a prudent and well-thought-out economic and political plan for the future of the United States in general and for the State of Florida in particular.

No matter how one looks at the economic and environmental woes plaguing this country, in essence they are simply costs of all kinds—costs that keep escalating and accelerating at the same time. Housing foreclosures, rising gasoline and food prices, unaffordable health care, accumulating credit card debt, collapse of the banking system, devaluation of the U.S. dollar, budget deficits, rising unemployment, products built with planned obsolescence and obsolete technologies, global warming, depletion of natural resources, natural disasters (such as hurricanes, earthquakes, floods, wildfires, and droughts), nuclear wastes, wars—all of these represent costs, either recurring, periodic, catastrophic, or of some other type.

What can we do about this plague of cost? We should—and can—get rid of it for good. But how can we do this when everything has a cost of some kind? By implementing the concept of a zero-cost economy, as presented in the following pages.

This blueprint can serve every country in the world, regardless of its specific economic and environmental conditions. The ultimate goal of a zero-cost economy is to create a cost-free and carefree economy—which I call *carefreeism*, defined as economic security in a carefree economy.

Carefreeism serves the general economic interests of all groups of people, from the impoverished to the superrich, without being politically tainted by any political party. It is a universally applicable concept. All political parties in the United States can and should adhere to the tenets of a zero-cost economy and carefreeism, because these can serve us all.

(*Note:* In this blueprint, the author repeats certain points to emphasize their importance and avoid misunderstandings or misinterpretations.)

The author of this blueprint plans to use the concept of a zero-cost economy as his political agenda to run for the Office of Governor of Florida during the forthcoming election.

Nobody knows for sure what the future will bring. However, I am confident that the concept of carefreeism must prevail to govern the economy of this great nation and of the rest of the world if the human race ultimately is to enjoy general economic security and prosperity in peace.

We encourage all Floridians, regardless of their political views or party affiliations, to energize themselves by getting acquainted with the concept of a zero-cost economy. If this movement prevails, Florida will become the economic and environmental "dream state" of the Union.

We are all Americans and must think and act like Americans before we subscribe to any ideology or political party. Cost is the biggest enemy of every American. Let's start the journey together to defeat cost and move towards creating a zero-cost economy.

PREFACE

The biggest and the most immediate threat to the U.S. economy is neither global warming nor the depletion of natural resources because the most dire effects of these events will not arise in the immediate future. (Experts believe we will not see the full impact of global warming for 50 to 100 years.) The most immediate peril we now face is the increase in costs of all types, all of them accelerating at the same time. If this devastating trend is not halted and reversed immediately, vigorously, and effectively, our good days will soon be over—for Florida and the rest of the nation.

How did we reach this critical point? We can place the blame on inept, imprudent, and shortsighted policies in all sectors—including the economy, energy, environment, and health care. We need not look far to realize this. Here are just a few examples: As of May 2008, Miami, Florida had more than 22,000 empty new condominiums without buyers and simultaneously was seeing record numbers of foreclosures. Needless to say, this reflects an unsound housing policy. The same trend is occurring in the rest of the state.

Runaway gasoline prices surely do not provide any kind of security for Floridians, much less a future. Even worse, no sound and effective energy policy is in sight.

The consequences of our failed healthcare policies are even worse for some people, potentially wiping out their life savings or causing financial ruin after a catastrophic illness or injury. Even greater devastation may await the 3.2 million Floridians without healthcare insurance. If such economic woes are compounded by food shortages and unaffordable food prices, chaos could occur, leading to a revolution of some sort. If you are skeptical, simply look back at history, which provides many examples of how revolutions begin. We must not let this happen.

Considering the nature of these and other policy failures in the United States, one concludes that the major cause is cost, which keeps escalating and accelerating simultaneously and continuously. With no examples of decreasing and decelerating cost, nothing exists to offset rising cost. An economy based on escalating and accelerating cost can only end in disaster, should disposable incomes fail to increase accordingly or, even worse, should they remain stagnant. The decrease in Americans' purchasing power will be compounded if we import goods with a devaluing currency, as shown by the rise in the cost of imported crude oil during much of 2008.

As bad as Florida's economic situation may be, the trend can be reversed. In fact, it can even be improved to the point where our state becomes the envy of the entire nation and even the world and serves as a viable model for other states and countries. Achieving this goal means reversing the trend of rising cost, which is the root cause of our economic problems. To do this, we must create a zero-cost economy in Florida.

Can an across-the-board, *absolute* zero-cost economy be achieved? No—a true zero-cost economy in *all* sectors is not possible. However, we can attain zero cost in many areas—most importantly, the critical areas of energy, transportation, environment, housing, education, communication, and health care. In sectors that cannot operate on a zero-cost basis (especially food and clothing), the overall effect of attaining zero cost in other areas would help decrease costs in those sectors.

To tackle cost, we must first freeze cost, then reduce it, and finally eliminate it altogether. Realizing a zero-cost economy in Florida will take plenty of hard work, understanding of the zero-cost concept, and a U-turn from current economic practices. But the effort will be worth it: Total implementation of a zero-cost economy can reward all of us for life by ushering in an era of general economic security.

Important: A zero-cost economy has nothing in common with the failed economic concepts of communism, socialism, and even, to some extent, capitalism. The zero-cost concept is best described as creating a carefree economy[1] in which general economic security is achieved—a kind of *general* capitalism, as opposed to the existing "elite capitalism" that dominates in the United States.

This blueprint explores the foundation for realizing a zero-cost economy in Florida, creating economic security in a carefree economy for every Floridian. When we reach this goal, we can enjoy living here with economic security like no other place on this planet—a true "American Dream" state.

Please join me as we start building a bright future that can be realized in our lifetimes—for all of us and our children.

Farid A. Khavari
May 17, 2008

---

1   This blueprint is based on a much longer, thoroughly researched work by Farid A. Khavari, to be published under the title *Carefreeism - Economic Security in a Carefree Economy.*

Chapter 1: YOUR FUTURE IS AT STAKE

Never before have Americans been at such a critical crossroad. And the future looks even bleaker, unless we do something serious—something more than just making empty promises and distributing handouts. What threatens us most as a nation is not global warming or depletion of our natural resources. Our biggest threat is rising costs, which are escalating and accelerating with each virtual breath we take.

Just look at the rising cost of gasoline and food. Add to that the chaos in the housing market. How much longer before we become a nation of illiterates because few of us can afford the cost of higher education? The economic situation does not need to get worse; it is already bad enough to make us start thinking seriously and demanding rigorous action. If we allow cost to keep rising unchallenged, all of us—including rich Americans—could go bankrupt.

Even if we are able to avoid that worst-case scenario, each day that goes by without attacking costs of all types we are taking a chance that the problem will be compounded and the cost of resolving it will rise even higher. In the process, as individuals and as a nation we will all become poorer—even the rich and superrich. But if we tackle cost immediately, we can avert this doomsday scenario.

Unfortunately, politicians are consumed with doing business as usual. Economists are not much better; they are not even in a position to find a better solution, almost as if their eyes are covered with blinders. They think cost is normal, a consequence of existence. The best solution most economists can come up with is to suggest tax breaks to stimulate the economy and create jobs.

But how much of a difference would a tax break of $500 or $1,000 a year make for poor and middle-class Americans? And what would a billionaire do if a tax break gave him an additional $10 million? Tax breaks are no more than a way to silence the poor with handouts or to enable the rich to extend their shamelessly extravagant lifestyles.

As this blueprint will describe in detail, there's a much better way to brighten our economic future—a way that avoids tax breaks and other failed methods. If tax breaks could work miracles, many Americans would not find themselves in the shape they are in today: unemployed or with stagnating incomes and declining purchasing power, increasingly falling victim to foreclosures, feeling frustrated and hopeless.

So we come to the main issue—economics. However, economics is intertwined with environmental issues. Making economic activities and needs compatible with environmental needs will require us to implement policies that cause little or no harm to the environment with the added benefit of bringing long-lasting economic gains.

However, when confronted with an economic problem, the politicians, economists, businesspeople, and practically everyone else seeks a piecemeal solution. The problem with a piecemeal solution is that it brings piecemeal results; a simple problem gets compounded and then returns to haunt us. A piecemeal solution is no more than a Band-Aid®. The correct and most effective approach is to seek a comprehensive solution that addresses all aspects of the economic and environmental spectrums. Achieving a zero-cost economy would do just that.

As Americans, we have two choices: Listen to the usual rhetoric and empty promises, or help achieve economic security as explained in this blueprint, which is based on sound, prudent economic and environmental policies. This is no trifling matter. Your own future—and your children's—are at stake.

Chapter 2: THE NEED FOR A COURSE CORRECTION

For a moment, imagine you live with your spouse and children in a log house far from immediate help. In the middle of a freezing night, you run out of every means to heat your home, except the logs it was built with. Would you burn those logs to keep from freezing to death? No question—you would burn everything that could produce heat to extend your survival, even for a short while longer, and avert death for yourself and your family.

Now imagine that just before you decide to burn the logs of your house, a continuous, never-ending supply of energy and heat arrives. Not only would you survive the night, but you would be able to live without the endless fear and worry that your fuel will run out. You would be looking at a bright future.

Now consider this: A billionaire is stuck in the middle of a desert with no source of hydration. His very life depends on his ability to get a single glass of water, yet nobody is available to deliver it to him. His billions of dollars cannot save him; they're worthless to him now because he has no access to the most basic requirement of life!

The concept of a zero-cost economy can help Floridians at all economic levels—poor, middle class, rich, and superrich. Of course, we cannot resolve all of our problems at the same time. But once we tackle the major issue—our dependency on energy (gasoline and electricity)—the others (such as housing, health care, Social Security, education, and property tax) can be adjusted much more easily.

But before we even think of becoming wealthy, we must put all our efforts into achieving cost-free living. Otherwise, it is just a matter of time before any amount of wealth we accumulate will be eaten away by rising cost, unless that wealth grows at a higher, faster pace as cost rises and accelerates. Cost-free living is the first and most important step toward accumulating true wealth, as this blueprint will explain.

1) INTRODUCTION

What kind of future can Americans in general and Floridians in particular look forward to? To answer this question, consider these issues:

- How far can anyone get when salaries do not keep pace with cost increases? In this situation, the purchasing power of a person's income declines steadily while costs of all types escalate and accelerate with no slowdown in sight.

- How much longer can the U.S. economy continue to depend on imported crude oil, considering that world oil reserves are shrinking and world demand keeps growing?

- How much longer can our economy afford to send hundreds of billions of dollars to unfriendly nations rich in crude oil without risking being crushed under the burden of deficits on the one hand and increased energy requirements and a higher cost of living on the other?

- How much longer can we keep polluting the environment by spewing carbon dioxide into the atmosphere before we can expect global warming to haunt us?

- Does anybody truly believe ethanol can be an effective solution to our crude-oil crisis? Moreover, why would we want to deplete nutritional materials from our agricultural land for the sake of obtaining ethanol?

- Undoubtedly, in the future the large majority of vehicles will have to be powered by electricity. However, two crucial questions must be answered:

   1) Which alternative energy technologies should be used to deliver this electricity?

   2) How should we power the tens of millions of existing vehicles now on the road in Florida and nationwide?

- Why should the CEOs of multinational companies (some of whom destroy the livelihoods of millions of working Americans by outsourcing jobs to other countries for the sake of profit and thereby cause devastating damage to the economy) earn salaries that are hundreds or thousands of times higher than those of the teachers who help our children learn and become useful members of society, or those of the engineers who develop technological solutions to our problems?

- How much longer can we continue to let the greedy exploit and ruin us financially, mentally, and emotionally and demand our corpses economically? In the past, American engineers were proud to carry calipers in their shirt pockets. Today, the most exciting thing for many Americans is to buy foreclosed properties or get into the business of financing, ruining people financially and compounding their woes!

- Who could remotely believe any politician who says he or she can provide long-term, universal healthcare insurance to all Floridians while ignoring escalating healthcare costs and failing to propose a solution?

- How can more than 9 million Floridians get halfway decent healthcare insurance when there is no end in sight to the cost-escalating race taking place among doctors, hospitals, lawyers, and insurance companies?

- How much longer will Americans have to work to replace shoddy products, second-rate vehicles, and inferior housing, all the while destroying our limited raw materials and causing environmental problems?

- Why has college education—a true reflection of the wealth of a person and a nation as a whole—become a luxury that many Americans cannot easily access?

- How much longer can we stand by and witness the inept, shallow policies that have raised property taxes in Florida, hounding some of us out of our homes or even out of our state and converting what could be a dream state to a ghost town and breeding ground for crime and robbery?

- What gives any finance company the right to foreclose homes on hardworking families simply because they lack an understanding of the quagmires of financing—and because of the greed of financial institutions?

- Why are credit card companies allowed to charge exorbitant interest rates and late fees, bilking money from Floridians? Why are they allowed to impose late fees at all, if interest is the cost of borrowed money?

- How secure are Floridians against such natural disasters as hurricane and tornadoes when the bases of the insurance companies in this state are built on shaky ground?

- How much longer can we watch Florida's accelerating decay and destruction from economic, environmental, and social forces before we decide to take stringent action?

It's high time we did something to stem our increasing economic woes. This blueprint, "Towards a Zero-Cost Economy," can lift country to a future brighter than we have ever imagined.

2) WHY A ZERO-COST ECONOMY?

If we could run an economy on a totally zero-cost basis, no economic or environmental problems would exist. However, this is not possible. In a modern economy, any kind of action has a cost—especially when nonrenewable energy sources and materials are used to manufacture products and goods with short life spans. As demand rises due to population growth and a higher standard of living, the race toward depletion of these resources escalates, unless interrupted by a recession.

Existing economic concepts do not offer a solution. This destructive trend cannot continue in a world where the cost of crude oil and other raw materials threatens to rise out of control for political, economical, technological, and environmental reasons on the one hand and due to speculative, exploitive, and manipulative drives on the other hand. The result will be nothing less than chaos and devastation. Even worse, any attempt to correct our present course becomes more difficult and exponentially more costly with each passing day. That is why we must take immediate action.

The needed course correction is to do everything possible to tackle our biggest enemy—cost of all types. Running an economy on the principle of zero cost is the *only* viable solution. The next chapter describes in detail the vicious cycle of cost and its devastating effects on the economy, environment, and the very existence of mankind.

As stated earlier, the biggest threat to mankind in general and to Americans in particular is not global warming, natural disasters, crude oil depletion, or the radical Islamic movement. It is escalating and accelerating cost. As long as the cost of a given item or service is low or manageable and can be paid, it is acceptable and tolerated. But the effects become devastating when the cost of any correction runs out of control. The goals of a zero-cost economy are to freeze costs initially, then reduce them, and finally (if possible) eliminate them altogether.

In plain English, a zero-cost economy means that if your income remains the same and does not increase:

- your purchasing power remains unchanged if the average cost of living is frozen

- your purchasing power increases if the average cost of living drops

- 100% of your purchasing power is at your disposal to spend or to save, creating true wealth, if costs are eliminated altogether.

3) WEALTH IN A ZERO-COST ECONOMY

The capitalist economic concept promotes individual ownership and as a result, wealth building. However, this is only temporary at best and for the overwhelming majority of people, it is an unrealizable dream.

On the other hand, average people living in capitalist economies (which seem to provide a better standard of living than socialist and communist economies) have achieved a higher standard of living by trading their free time for material gains. This has accomplished at an enormous cost to irreplaceable natural resources, devastating the environment.

Ironically, the pursuit of wealth in a capitalist economic system is not just an unending endeavor. Even for the wealthiest people, pursuing wealth is not a long-lasting, stable situation. Wealth cannot be stable or long-lasting when exposed to the permanent loss of purchasing power and/or value. Furthermore, how can wealth survive in an economy based on speculation, greed, and manipulation? Few of us have sufficient knowledge to withstand

and survive a financial environment rife with speculation, greed, and manipulation. In the end, everybody loses.

How can one build wealth in a zero-cost economy when average costs are increasing at a higher pace than income?

Nobody can build wealth in the following circumstances:

- Your total income stagnates while your total costs increase.

- You get hit by a huge unexpected cost, as from a lawsuit, a major illness, or a divorce.

- You fall victim to a natural disaster, fire, or crime (unless you have adequate insurance coverage).

- You live above your financial means and become a victim of interest and gouging.

- You end up outliving your savings.

In contrast, a zero-cost economy can help you achieve the following results:

- If your living costs can be frozen totally, your purchasing power will remain stable. Although you will not be able to accumulate wealth, you will not become poor, either. You will still need to work for the required time to maintain your income level.

- If you can reduce your living costs partially or totally, your purchasing power will increase even if your income remains stagnant. In this case, you could choose either to keep working the same number of hours and end up saving money, or cut back on your working hours.

- If you can eliminate all costs and live practically cost free, you can start saving all your income to build wealth, or stop working and simply start enjoying life. With such zero-cost living, you can accumulate wealth to spend on the additional expenses of a leisure society (which are not

11

covered with zero-cost living). For example, you could travel by air (assuming you do not own your own private plane, which can be flown with a free source of energy).

Do not confuse a leisure society such as the one a zero-cost economy could create with a lifestyle based on mere traveling and parties. A healthy, progress-oriented leisure society is more diverse and promotes education, innovation, research and development, and many other constructive activities. The societal values that shape such a society and the results derived from them will create a bright future for our economy, because human talents and energy will be used toward mankind's progress. But if we continue to suffer under rising costs caused by increasing economic woes and environmental limitations, the sorry end of mankind cannot be far away.

4) ECONOMIC CONDITIONS IN A ZERO-COST ECONOMY

Whether an economic system is capitalist or socialist, a devastating phenomenon occurs: Costs increase while purchasing power undergoes a permanent decline, as graph #1 (on the next page) clearly shows. Although this graph depicts stagnating incomes with permanently increasing costs, a similar decline in purchasing power accompanied by increasing debt occurs with increasing incomes if those incomes don't grow faster than costs. In an inflationary economy, purchasing power declines regardless of income increases; in other words, the purchasing power of a dollar (or other currency) decreases rather than stays the same.

Graph # 1: Typical economic conditions in a capitalistic economic system

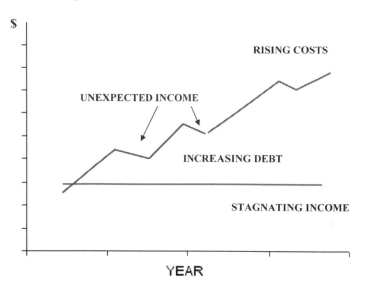

Savings and wealth can't accumulate unless purchasing power increases. But how can we achieve this goal? Normally, purchasing power can be improved either through steady increases in income (which must always exceed costs) or through cost reduction, even if incomes stagnate. Logically, a simultaneous rise in incomes along with cost reduction would boost purchasing power that much more. To be clear, cost reduction shouldn't be achieved at the expense of a decreased standard of living. On the contrary, it must be achieved by *improving* the standard of living, as this book will explain.

Initially, a zero-cost economy may seem to be deflationary. However, this appearance is deceiving. Because, a conventional deflationary economy is marked by a shortage of money and credit, declining inventory, dropping prices, increasing unemployment, a stagnating economy, and massive bankruptcies, which can ravage the economy even more than inflation can. In this situation, the economy and the people are virtually broke—poised at the edge of the proverbial cliff.

In a zero-cost economy, on the other hand, people own their homes, automobiles, and everything else while living in a carefree economy. They're not riding a rollercoaster economy subject to booms and busts. They enjoy a carefree economic security, as described in this book.

As graph #2 (below) shows, the beauty of a zero-cost economy is that it creates true wealth, which brings economic security and paves the way for a transition to a leisure- and knowledge-based society. As a result, economic slavery doesn't exist and people start enjoying life without the burden of daily financial pressures. However, if we fail to increase general purchasing power by controlling costs, economic security will elude us. By itself, creating new jobs can't achieve this important goal.

Graph # 2: Economic conditions in a zero-cost economy

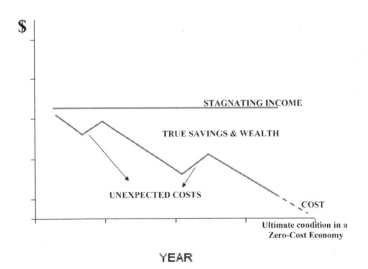

5) ECONOMIC SECURITY INDICES AS INDICATORS OF ECONOMIC WELL-BEING

The Gross Domestic Product (GDP)[2] is considered the yardstick by which to measure all goods and services that a nation produces over a 1-year period. If the GDP in the previous year shows growth—let's say 3% growth over the previous year—politicians tend to go on a spending binge without realizing these figures are distorted. As a result, a huge scam begins to take shape. The following example should clarify what I mean:

You have $1,000 in your checking account. You pay $200 for a doctor's visit and $50 for the prescribed medicine. As you're being examined in the doctor's office, a vehicle damages the passenger-side mirror on your car, which is parked outside the office. Replacing the mirror costs $400. When balancing your checkbook, you subtract $650 ($200 for the doctor's visit + $50 for the prescription + $400 for car repair) from your starting balance of $1,000. This leaves just $350 in your checking account.

---

2   The author was among the first critics of the GDP and the conventional concept of economic growth. His thoughts began to take shape as early as 1971 during a seminar for advanced economics at the University of Hamburg in Germany, which compared the different economic growth models, including the Solow model. Being a foreign student in Germany was not easy; getting into a heated discussion with a German professor during his seminar was simply intolerable—especially when the professor was Dr. H. Todt. In 1991, the author decided to write about his criticism of the GDP as part of a book. (See Khavari, Farid A.: *Environomics – The Economics of Environmentally Safe Prosperity*; Praeger: Westport, CT and London; 1993, p. 26 ff.) One of the better approaches to dealing with the GDP's deficiencies is to replace the GDP with the Genuine Progress Indicator (GPI), which combines the concepts of "green" economics and welfare economics. Redefining Progress, an Oakland, California think tank, created the GPI in 1995.

Now, what would happen if you mistakenly *added* (instead of subtracted) those three expenditures to your starting balance of $1,000? Your checkbook would show an incorrect amount of $1,650 ($1,000 + $200 + $50 + $400). If you believe you have $1,650 instead of $350 in your checking account and you start spending accordingly, you will be in a big trouble. All of your checks beyond $350 will bounce.

Believe it or not, economists calculate the GDP the latter way. They *add* rather than *deduct* healthcare, environmental, maintenance, and military expenditures and the costs incurred from natural disasters. This creates a situation resembling an overdrawn checking account.

The fact is, any type of cost is just a cost. When you pay for health care, for instance, you gain nothing except better health (if the care succeeds). The false perception of economic growth initiates a vicious cycle of exploitation and destruction: Everyone goes on a binge of demanding more and spending more. In reality, they are spending something that does not exist as value, only as a cost—a social cost. Social costs are costs related to health care, environmental restoration, wars, natural disasters, and the like. They yield no improvement other than to restore something to its original condition.

So what is the *right* way to calculate the GDP? To get a true figure, one must deduct all costs and must consider everything a cost unless some gains have been achieved (which could reflect growth). For instance, if a house is destroyed by a hurricane and replaced with a new one, the value of the new house should not be added to the GDP unless some kind of value was added to the house. Even more critical is the possibility that the old house was paid off in full but lacked wind insurance coverage. Because the homeowner now must borrow money to rebuild the house, it should be considered a loss; the original house (which was paid off) should be deducted from the GDP or any other measure of a nation's economic well-being.

In other words, to use a sound accounting method to calculate the GDP, we would deduct the value of the old house from the total GDP, because it represents a loss. But this is not the way government economists think, because it is complicated and practically impossible to do this successfully. In addition, they would have to adjust the amount if the house was paid off. If the old house were not lost due to a natural disaster and materials for the replacement house were used to build a new house, it would have been a gain.

Obviously, then, the GDP does not reveal useful data. For a responsible government, there is a much better way to measure economic well-being, monitor progress or decline, and try to improve things. For an accruement measurement, we must use methods that compare the economic progress of all people in every possible area of the economy; the GDP is worthless in that regard. We must measure economic progress in real and tangible terms that document changes based on progress or declines made by each individual, household, community, city, and state.

For this purpose, we must introduce a totally new method, called Economic Security Indices (ESI)[3], which measures data in the following categories:

---

3   The term Economic Security Indices (ESI) is being introduced here for the first time as a sound method of calculating economic progress and well-being. A detailed description of the ESI is presented in: Khavari, Farid A. *Carefreeism – Economic Security in a Carefree Economy.* Of course, efforts have been made in the past to correct the GDP's shortcomings. As a result, the terms Green Gross Domestic Product and Genuine Progress Indicator (GPI) were developed; however, these concepts themselves have various shortcomings. For details, see *Carefreeism.*

- number of households that purchased a home or condominium compared to the year before

- number of people who paid off or lowered their mortgages compared to the previous year

- number of people who had healthcare coverage compared to the previous year

- number of people who became healthier or sicker compared to the previous year

- number of people who completed their higher education compared to the previous year

- number of people who received a free college and postgraduate education compared to the previous year

- number of houses and other buildings converted to alternative energy sources and becoming totally independent of centralized energy facilities, compared to the previous year

- number of vehicles powered by solar or wind energy at zero cost compared to the previous year

- number of vehicles converted from gas to electric power compared to the previous year

- number of people who accumulated savings compared to the previous year

- number of people who retired from working life before age 65 (moving toward a leisure society) compared to the previous year

- average hours worked per week compared to the previous year. (*Note:* With a zero-cost economy, there is a trade-off between accumulating wealth and having more free time or decreasing the number of work hours. The more hours worked, the more wealth a person can accumulate in real terms.)

- social costs (such as from health care, environmental problems, legal problems, and similar costs) compared to the previous year.

Once such data have been gathered, economists could compare progress or decline and the nation could work toward improvement. The higher the positive numbers, the greater the economic progress, in real and tangible terms, that has been achieved.

Such measurements would be used for every sector of the economy. Once a certain level of success was achieved for the overwhelming majority of Americans, policies would be implemented to improve living conditions further.

This begs the question: How can we improve our economic well-being? The answer: By implementing the concept of a zero-cost economy.

6) GENERAL CAPITALISM THROUGH A ZERO-COST ECONOMY

The primary goal of a capitalist economic system with a free market economy is to maximize profit in the interest of businesses and their owners and shareholders. The interests of the general public or consumers are secondary, important only if they generate more profit for businesses. Profit maximizing is short term in nature; long-term goals get little attention because they eat into profits.

In a capitalist system, businesses not only seek to maximize profit but strive to ensure the continuity of profit maximizing— thus, creating recurring cost for consumers. For the consumer, a recurring cost is a repeated cost; for a business, the recurring cost for the consumer is recurring income or repeated income. For a business to maintain a recurring income (the foundation of profit maximizing), it must incorporate planned obsolescence into its products, make its products dependent on certain resources (such as gasoline to power vehicles), or emphasize centralization (as with centralized power plants). For the consumer, using gasoline to fuel vehicle costs money; however, for oil companies, it is a repeated source of income. The same concept applies to power plants; consumers pay every month to use power.

Pursuing the goal of maximizing profit requires tough measures that in the long run create a growing inequality which contributes to general poverty due to declining purchasing power. This negative effect can worsen when U.S. jobs are outsourced to low-cost-labor countries—a practice that increases profit for businesses (although only in the relative short term). Such outsourcing decreases the purchasing power of potential future buyers of goods and services. Although outsourcing jobs or reducing employees' work hours can help a business maintain a profit, such profit-maximizing efforts are welcome only if they do not come at the expense of working people.

This author believes that a company should be allowed to outsource jobs and the government should allow outsourcing or work-hour reductions *only* in these circumstances:

- to find replacement jobs for workers whose jobs have been outsourced or whose working hours have been cut, thus preventing loss of income for these workers

- to follow the principles of a zero-cost economy with the goal of protecting citizens' economic well-being and purchasing power.

Furthermore, a responsible government must protect businesses from falling victim to their own greed and profit-maximizing drive. To make it perfectly clear: A corporation's drive to maximize profit forces it to spend money (a profit-reducing measure) in the interest of research and development (R & D) so it can improve its products and develop new ones. Problems caused by pursuing maximum profits can be compounded not only through a company's resistance to costly R & D work but also through legislation. Industry lobbyists influence legislators from the local and state levels all the way to the federal level. It should come as no surprise that our vehicles get poor gas mileage or that decentralized solar systems have not been rigorously implemented in this country; in large part, we have lobbyists to blame.

As a result, businesses start to suffer, as the following examples show: Although Toyota was a virtual nonentity in the automobile industry three decades earlier, it overtook (or came close to overtaking) General Motors, the world's largest car manufacturer, in sales by making more efficient vehicles. European Airbus, a start-up aerospace company four decades ago, has overtaken the mighty Boeing. And where are yesteryear's airline giants— Eastern and Pan Am? Out of business.

The decline and even demise of corporations matters little to the rich and superrich. Our present political system is not based on the principles of democracy. Instead, it is a plutocracy—a political system indirectly governed by a relatively small group of the rich and superrich, whom I call elite capitalists. Their foundation can be traced back to the profit-maximizing drive. To counter this trend and in the interest of creating general capitalists without jeopardizing elite capitalists' interests, we need to move to a zero-cost economy.

Achieving a zero-cost economy means implementing economic policies that, at minimum, freeze costs to the extent possible in all areas of the economy. Secondly, we must make every attempt to reduce every cost that can possibly be reduced. The last and final step is to eliminate all costs that possibly can be eliminated. These efforts are discussed in more detail later.

7) CHANGING ROLE OF THE ELITE CAPITALISTS

As just described, the United States is ruled indirectly by a plutocracy of the rich and superrich—the elite capitalists. Many things, both good and bad, can be attributed to elite capitalists. For instance, they create jobs (a good thing), yet they exploit the economy (a bad thing). We can either fight them or implement economic and political policies that make good use of their resources, talents, and power to set a sound economic foundation that creates general capitalists based on a zero-cost economy. We can also help elite capitalists do the right things by guiding them in the right direction. In short, we must turn them into valuable assets.

Fighting the elite capitalists would be as grave a mistake as caving in to them. Conservatives propose giving them tax cuts of all kinds to motivate them to invest. For reasons that will be explained shortly, this idea is nonsense. The rich and superrich do not invest out of love for the people; nor are they in the business of charity to provide jobs. They invest because it gives them the chance to make and maximize profits. Tax cuts would not enhance their willingness to invest if they see an opportunity to make and maximize profit; conversely, lack of tax cuts would not make them less willing to invest in those circumstances.

On the other hand, many liberals demand higher taxes for the rich and superrich in the hope of creating some fairness and to finance what they see as much-needed projects. They also promote tax cuts for the poor and middle class on the grounds that doing this would stimulate the economy and help those groups.

In reality, though, giving tax cuts to the poor and middle class would have little effect. The poor would gain practically nothing, because they pay little or no taxes. The middle class would reap an extra few hundred or, at most, an extra thousand dollars each year—not enough to make a dramatic difference, except perhaps to pay the interest on their mortgage payment or reduce their credit card balance for a month or two.

So the question remains: What effective actions can we take that would make sense for all groups—the poor, middle class, rich, and superrich? Certainly, we should *not* favor one economic class against another, as this would be a waste of energy and resources. On the contrary, we should give elite capitalists the incentive to accomplish certain goals; then, once they've accomplished these goals, we should reward them. It's important, though, that we withhold their rewards until they have met the desired goals. We should guide elite capitalists and other entrepreneurs in the right direction in the interests of the economy and the environment. They would enjoy all the pleasures of profit maximizing as long as they did the things the right way, as described below.

Let's assume our economic condition demands a policy to immediately convert gas-powered vehicles to electric-powered vehicles (with solar energy powering electric vehicles, at least in Florida). The government could provide a series of incentives, such as the following three options:

1. **A tax exemption from income and/or profit for a certain time period**—let's say 10 to 20 years from the date the policy is announced. To promote the success of this policy, the tax exemption or loss of potential dividend write-offs from income tax could be extended to the company's shareholders for the period of R & D work, to stimulate the effort toward realizing the designated project to its full potential. This measure would not cost the government a single penny, because the involved product or technology previously did not exist and thus did not generate any tax revenue to begin with. Thus, the government would reach an economic goal within a given time period because

the company would strive to achieve the goal as soon as possible and thus benefit longer from the tax exemption (helping to maximize profit). Once the project was in full production, the government would collect income tax not just from the company's employees but also from its supplying companies and their employees (as well as others in a booming economy). At the same time, the worry associated with unemployment and potential recession (not to mention economic woes) would dissolve.

2. **A sales tax exemption for the products sold.** Exempting sales tax for products associated with the designated project would promote sales and contribute to the company's profit-maximizing goal. Although sales of those products would not generate tax revenue, they would indirectly increase revenues through tax revenues generated by the sale of other products in a booming economy (an effect of consumers' increased purchasing power). Loss of sales tax revenue for these products should not deter the government from pursuing such a policy, because revenue derived from sales of those products did not exist in the first place. However, this step would create the potential for future tax revenue once the tax exemption expired. In the meantime, the economic goals would be realized.

3. **Refunding the cost of R & D or rewarding certain accomplishments.** This would be the last option, because it would cost the government money. But it would certainly be more effective and less expensive than such measures as tax cuts with no performance requirement attached. Costs to the government would come only after the company reached the designated goal; the government would not lose money if the project failed. (*Note:* Giving rewards such as tax cuts in advance, before a company accomplishes a goal, would be an almost-total failure. There should be no prize without sweat.)

If these options were not enough to entice elite capitalists to achieve the desired goals, what choices would they have to survive in an environment of declining consumer purchasing power? Until now, their options have included "bubbles" in the real estate market, banking and credit industries, and automotive industry. Sooner or later, though, all bubbles burst and the general population grows poorer. When a nation's middle class starts to decline, next in line are the rich and then the handful of superrich—the elite capitalists. Remember—wealth is worth having and accumulating only if it can be used to get desired products and services. Should these products and services disappear, wealth eventually would be worthless, especially if the wealthy have accounts in banks that are in trouble or are invested heavily in real estate at a time when foreclosures are soaring. Wealth also counts for little when no factories are left to manufacture goods and no facilities are left to provide services. At that point, the superrich will cease to exist.

8) SUBSTITUTION OF CRUDE OIL: THE OVERLOOKED LINK

Energy experts and economists continually assure us that if the price of crude oil keeps rising, alternative energy sources eventually will replace crude oil. They cite the basic economic theory that one type of good can be substituted for another, as far as the two types can be consumed or used in place of one or another for at least some of their possible uses. Here are two typical misleading assumptions:

- If oil prices continue to rise, alternative energy sources will replace crude oil.

- As the production volume of alternative energy sources (such as solar and wind energy) increases, related industries will reach "grid parity," meaning the cost of producing the alternative energy will be comparable to the cost of obtaining electricity from crude oil or any other fossil fuels.[4]

But a closer analysis shows that a series of steps and considerations must be taken to initiate efficient substitution of crude oil with alternative energy sources; rising price is just one of many factors even if, in some cases, it turns out to be an important one. Here are a few scenarios related to the first assumption:

• Let's say the Organization of the Petroleum Exporting Countries (OPEC) abruptly set the price of crude oil at $1,000 or even $2,000 per barrel. The substitution theory assumes that substituting crude oil with other energy sources could be done easily and immediately. Unfortunately, this is not true, because sufficient amounts of immediate alternatives are lacking. Not only would substitution *not* take place; even worse, the world economy (which depends heavily on oil) would collapse overnight if an oil shortage occurred or if oil was withdrawn for political or economic reasons. The result would be an economic disaster of unimaginable magnitude. If crude oil stopped flowing because of high prices, few people would be able to afford it, as in the 2008 oil price increase. Unless oil were substituted with an alternative energy source, the world economy would collapse. On the other hand, rising oil prices would not trigger an automatic substitution process, as most people assume. In other words, we must initiate the substitution process regardless of whether we are to become oil-independent. It does not matter if the efforts toward oil independence come from domestic or foreign sources. Rising oil prices will not start

---

4   Waters, Richard and Harvey, Fiona: Squeeze is on as interest grows in solar sector. *Financial Times,* London, England. June 8, 2008, p. 19.

the market mechanism for substitution of crude oil unless we implement an aggressive energy policy.

• Suppose crude oil prices rose gradually and permanently. Even so, effective substitution would not occur unless the country implemented a rigorous energy policy to substitute crude oil with alternative energy sources and technologies. The belief that rising oil prices would accelerate substitution is not realistic even in a fully functioning market economy[5], which serves as a basic assumption. If oil prices rise, the demand for crude decreases, as long as the possibility of substitution exists. Decreasing prices influence the substitution process; at the same time, energy consumption rises so that oil prices, in the end, fluctuate cyclically with an upward tendency. In other words, rising oil prices would have a limited effect, at best, on crude oil substitution from a microeconomic standpoint if companies or private households (due to cost comparisons) prefer one energy source over another. However, from a macroeconomic perspective, rising prices would not initiate an effective substitution process. When oil prices keep rising, the demand for oil drops; as a result, the price of oil drops. This process will continue indefinitely unless oil substitution occurs: the market-price-mechanism (in which oil prices increase when the demand exceeds supply and decrease when the supply exceeds demand) does not apply to oil. Therefore, we must implement oil substitution without any expectation from the market-price-mechanism. During 2008, oil prices rose from about $25 per barrel to $160 and then dropped down to $60. Similarly, gasoline prices went up $1 per gallon to $4.80 and then fell to $2.50.

---

5   Khavari, Farid A.: Prerequisites for an efficient substitution of crude oil, in: *Ekonomska Analiza,* Belgrade, Yugoslavia. 1976, p. 272.

Effective substitution of crude oil with alternative energy sources would involve a series of vital factors, as follows:

1) Achieving total substitution of crude oil requires availability of substitute energy sources and technologies that can provide enough energy to replace crude oil, both quantitatively (as an energy source) and qualitatively (as a source of raw materials). Solar, wind, or nuclear energy can be used to generate electricity for heating and cooling purposes but not to replace gas to run cars, except vehicles designed to run on electricity. Substituting crude oil as a source of raw material is of less concern with regard to energy; the raw material portion of crude can be replaced by such sources as tar sand, oil shale, and coal.

2) Time is an important factor. A major project such as a centralized power plant (whether for solar, wind, nuclear, or any other energy source) takes a relatively long period to implement—usually 10 to 15 years or even longer from start of the project until it is ready to deliver energy. Thus, a project of this magnitude should be undertaken only as a last resort in areas where decentralized energy systems cannot be used.

3) Practically speaking, the rising costs of centralized energy plants are more concerning than their technological challenges (the latter of which are the biggest drawback). Experience shows that nobody can calculate such costs accurately—a situation typically resulting in tremendous cost overruns that make the entire enterprise questionable.

4) Technological obsolescence is a major issue for centralized power plants, considering how long it takes to build them—especially if new technology is developed but cannot be integrated into the system. In this case, the plant must operate with the older

technology until it becomes technologically or economically inoperable

5) Centralized energy plants pose concerns about safety and lack of protection from manmade or natural disasters, such as tsunamis, hurricanes, earthquakes, and technical failures. For instance, nuclear power plants can experience meltdowns, causing a disaster similar to the one at Chernobyl in 1986. Other types of problems at centralized plants may lead to power blackouts, such as the New York City blackout of August 2003 and the Miami blackouts of February 2008 (caused by technological problems) and October 2005 (caused by Hurricane Wilma, which effectively put Florida out of business for more than 20 days). Can you imagine what the death toll might have been had the New York City power outage occurred during a frigid winter? Similarly, if a natural disaster knocked out the Turkey Point nuclear power plant in Homestead (a Miami suburb), the entire state would be catapulted back to the Stone Age.

6) The challenge of substituting crude oil with other energy sources could be compounded, leading to failure if replacement energy sources are chosen without thorough analysis. For instance, ethanol cannot contribute to effective substitution of crude oil, either quantitatively or qualitatively. Also, its promotion could drain financial resources from efforts to develop more promising energy sources. Furthermore, use of land to grow agricultural products that produce ethanol could deplete such land of valuable nutritional material. It could also contribute to higher food prices and delay energy substitution by making future substitution more expensive and difficult by diverting attention and resources for dealing with compounded and escalated economic challenges.

29

7) Nonetheless, a delay in or rising costs of oil substitution will have devastating effects on the economy, imposing an economic burden that could be many times higher than the initial cost of substitution. The rising cost of running an economy also would increase the cost of substitution and impose additional social costs due to the accelerating nature of the costs.

8) The transition period from crude to an alternative energy source must be considered. Although energy conservation would help, it has its limits. For instance, people can save gas by driving less, which would lower the demand for gas. But such conservation measures would bring benefits only if no additional demands are created, as through an increased number of vehicles or a greater demand for gas in other sectors of the economy, either nationally or internationally. We must also determine how to power existing vehicles once we have switched to an alternative energy source (whether it is electricity generated by solar power or windmills or by hydrogen directly). And we must decide if existing gas-powered vehicles should be converted to electricity. These and similar issues must be dealt with.

9) Each alternative energy source and technology has its own environmental implications. The difficult task is not so much in choosing the source (or sources) with the fewest environment effects but in dealing with the political and economic interests of the various power brokers and interest groups. This decision should not discourage us from making the right choice as to which energy source to substitute for crude oil.

Considering the many disadvantages of centralized energy plants, decentralized energy delivery must be a top priority when determining policy for developing and implementing alternative energy sources. As I will explain later, decentralized delivery is less challenging and more beneficial than centralized energy delivery in every way. It can be installed and start providing energy in a matter of days or, with a larger system, in a matter of weeks. If a natural disaster were to knock out the decentralized solar or wind energy systems for thousands of households, the next day hundreds of thousands of other households would be in operation. In contrast, if such a disaster destroyed a centralized energy plant, the entire community would be put out of service—possibly permanently.

Once these and other relevant and crucial issues are considered and effective solutions are implemented, the issue of grid parity will make sense and can become a valid topic of debate—but not before then.

In light of these facts, it would be extremely naive to believe that rising crude oil prices will allow efficient substitution of crude oil simply through market-price mechanisms. Instead, substitution will require a rigorous, effective energy policy based on the principles described above. The sooner such a policy is implemented, the less such substitution will cost.

Chapter 3: THE PROBLEM OF COST

There are two things everyone should avoid: One is the plague and the second is cost—cost of all types. Just as the plague imperils one's health, cost jeopardizes the economic existence of all citizens, rich and poor. Disease and pestilence do not differentiate between the rich and the poor. Although the poor and the middle class may begin to suffer first, the rich and superrich will soon follow unless costs are brought under total control. History is full of examples. Once inflation, recession, and economic chaos occur, revolution may be just around the corner.

Therefore, cost is the first economic factor that must be controlled totally. This section explains why cost has such a devastating impact on the economy.

1) THE VICIOUS CYCLE OF COST

Cost not only escalates but also accelerates to the point where no increase in income can catch up with it—especially for people who live on their salaries. Even worse, a single cost compounds with the profit margin. That means one must pay a set percentage as profit on the incurred cost of that product. Cost escalation varies with the number of stages a product goes through until it reaches the end-consumer. In the case of energy, cost compounds just like interest on money.

For example, assume that the energy used to manufacture a given product costs $10, that this product goes through five stages before it reaches the end-consumer, and that during each stage, a 10% profit is added to its cost. As a result, the ultimate cost of the energy needed to make the product is $16.11, not $10—a whopping 62% increase.

This example shows how an increase in energy costs affects just a single product. Consider a similar effect on the thousands of consumer products and services available. Also consider how consumers' costs would rise if the cost of other raw materials used to make that same product also rose. Ultimately, the result would be a decline in general purchasing power, putting us on the fast track to poverty.

The same actions and consequences take place in many other areas of the economy with different products and services, while the salaries and incomes of the general population remain stagnant or increase too slowly to catch up with the general cost increase. The result is a permanent decline in purchasing power, with eventual economic collapse on the horizon.

2) DIFFERENT TYPES OF COST

To stop the vicious cycle of cost, we need to understand the different types of cost. By definition, cost is a bad thing because it eats into our earnings and savings. It can also ruin a person, a community, or a nation if imprudent economic policies are implemented and financial decisions are flawed.

Generally, four types of cost exist:

- **Permanently recurring cost.** This type of cost recurs again and again on a daily, weekly, or monthly basis. It includes such items as food, rent, mortgage, clothing, energy, insurance, transportation, interest, taxes (on sales and income), and maintenance or repair work.

- **Periodically occurring cost.** This type of cost occurs at monthly, yearly, or less frequent intervals. Some periodic costs occur only during certain decades in one's life. Periodically occurring costs include the cost of college education, vacations, and retirement.

- **Catastrophic costs.** Typically one-time events, these costs include unexpected medical bills; legal fees associated with divorce, malpractice, or similar events; accidents; disability due to disease or accident; and damages caused by natural disasters. Subprime loans and mortgages also fall into this category.

- **Social costs:** These costs are related to health care, the environment, maintenance, depletion of natural resources and agricultural land, and criminal lawsuits.

Some of these costs affect people directly, while others (primarily social costs) have indirect effects. Similarly, some are microeconomic factors (pertaining to individuals, companies, and industries) while others are macroeconomic (pertaining to whole systems). Nonetheless, we must find ways—economically, politically, technologically, or through all three avenues—to get to the root of all costs. Next, we must make every attempt to freeze costs, reduce them, and finally eliminate them altogether.

Conventionally, increased costs are transferred to the next person or company in one of two ways:

- vertically, as when a company passes its cost increases on to the next company, and so on, until the increase reaches the consumer

- horizontally, as when an oil company passes its cost increases on to manufacturers and suppliers of raw materials.

Increases in the cost of products and services drive workers to ask for salary increases. Thus, unless efforts are made to reduce costs, it is a losing game all the way around. To put it another way, there would be no need to increase one's income if the cost of living were reduced or, ideally, eliminated altogether. As costs start to decline, the purchasing power of a given income level will rise and social costs will decrease due to declining environmental damage and a decreased need for nonrenewable natural resources.

3) IS AN ABSOLUTE ZERO-COST-ECONOMY POSSIBLE?

If an economy could be run with absolutely zero costs, we would not have the economic, environmental, political, religious, racial, or other problems we face today. Unfortunately, a 100% zero-cost economy is not possible.

However, this should not discourage us, because any gain in cost containment is a tremendous step toward realizing a zero-cost economy. Also, keep in mind that many costs can be eliminated by individual households if they begin better planning. Elimination of other costs will require the vision and efforts of politicians to channel developments in the proper direction.

To start implementing a zero-cost economy, we must:

- eliminate all costs that recur on a permanent or periodic basis, such as those related to energy, transportation, rent, mortgage, interest, tuition, and retirement

- reduce all costs that cannot be eliminated, such as insurance, health care, maintenance and repair, and social costs brought about by environmental degradation and natural resource depletion.

Taxes also can be reduced if we implement prudent economic and political policies based on sound technological development. However, governments at all levels require revenue to pay for their services. Some of this can come from direct sales (such as the sale of stamps by the U.S. Postal Service), by charging fines for traffic and other violations, and by issuing professional licenses. Other services cannot be paid for simply by charging fees; this category includes entertainment for military troops and the costs of social services that governments commonly provide. Thus, taxes become necessary to a government's existence. Government needs revenue, and this can—and must—be attained through taxes.

4) BREAKING OUT OF THE VICIOUS CYCLE OF COST

Achieving a zero-cost economy will call for a series of well-measured economic, fiscal, political, and technological policies. It would be a disaster to try to reach this goal by mimicking the CEOs of some corporations, who can think of no way to cut costs other than firing employees, downsizing, and outsourcing production to low-cost-labor countries. These methods may generate profits for corporations and their shareholders but ultimately are destructive and cause the middle class—the most important base of an economy—to break down, shrink, and disappear.

But if cost-cutting measures such as firing, downsizing, and outsourcing are poor choices, what is the alternative solution? The first and foremost goal of any economic-political policy must be to avoid the conventional method of increasing poverty in the interest of maximizing profit. This method is wrong socially because no one should have the right to damage another's livelihood for the sake of profit. In addition, it is shortsighted because in the long run, everyone loses, even the rich and superrich.

No one would deny that the rich and superrich should be able to enjoy life in an environment of peace, prosperity, and security. Maximizing profit in an environment of uncertainty and at any expense should be given low priority. Acquiring wealth through methods that make others poor and homeless is no great achievement. Instead, the trick is to make others well-off while accumulating wealth for oneself.

The vicious cycle of cost is paralyzing our economy. To break out of this cycle, we need to achieve a zero-cost economy, which entails freezing costs, reducing them, and finally eliminating them altogether wherever possible. Energy is the most devilish cost and must be eliminated—totally, rigorously, and permanently—before we can tackle any other cost. The cost of energy, whether for private households or corporations, is the plague of our economy.

Why must we tackle the cost of energy first? Because it is the root source of the vicious cycle of cost. The cost of energy does not just escalate and accelerate as energy goes through the different production stages until reaching the consumer. It also causes these negative effects:

- It reduces the purchasing power of private households, companies, and governments.

- As the cost of energy rises, the entire economy becomes less mobile, leading to a decline in economic activity and eventually to a recession.

- The increasing cost of imported energy (crude oil) leads to increased deficits, which the cost of interest compounds further.

- Unemployment rises as the cost of energy escalates.

- Rising energy costs put America's wealth at risk of ending up in the hands of hostile Middle Eastern countries.

- The future cost of developing alternative energy sources becomes tremendously more expensive.

- Social costs stemming from environmental degradation and depletion of natural resources (crude oil) increase.

- Ultimately, the United States will lose its economic, technological, and military superiority in the world.

No other type of cost comes with such severe consequences. Therefore, the first and most crucial step towards a zero-cost economy is to reduce energy costs mercilessly. This will channel our economy in the right direction and give it a bright future such as we have never experienced.

Chapter 4: HOW TO ACHIEVE A ZERO-COST ECONOMY

Undoubtedly, achieving a zero-cost economy will mean slashing costs. However, it is immensely important to understand the right way to do this. We must use all available economic, political, technological, and environmental measures to make a zero-cost economy possible.

Of course, we cannot slash all costs from top to bottom in every sector of the economy simultaneously or arbitrarily. We will need to take a graduated approach, especially as we intend to reverse a process that has built up over many decades. This chapter describes a prudent approach to achieving a zero-cost economy.

1) ECONOMIC SECURITY THROUGH A ZERO-COST ECONOMY

For most Americans, the general perception of how to live a prosperous life is to work, and work, and keep working—a process akin to a death sentence that's prolonged until the gallows are placed around one's neck. No matter what a person does or how much wealth one accumulates, there's no such thing as economic security in the United States. You can pay off your house, but if you fail to pay property taxes on it, eventually it will be auctioned off. Similarly, if you miss several mortgage payments, your house will be foreclosed.

This is the cruel reality of our economy: It does not matter how much wealth you accumulate or if you pay off your home, you still cannot have peace of mind that your home will not be taken away. In America, economic security is a mirage. Even the richest of the rich cannot rest easily.

Dwelling on the root cause of this problem would take us far off course from the main topic of this blueprint. To achieve the general idea, think back to the Enron scandal, in which corporate wrongdoing wiped out the company's investors. In reality, no company is safe—not even such Wall Street giants as Bear Stearns, Lehman Brothers, Merrill Lynch, AIG, and Washington Mutual, all of which went under in 2008. If you look closely, you can see that cost was the main reason for their downfall. Of course, such factors as greed, manipulation, and dishonesty also can contribute to a corporation's demise. Ultimately, cost—and the increasing economic insecurity that goes along with it—is to blame.

You may be wondering: How can a zero-cost economy bring economic security? In an economy such as our present one, in which cost keeps escalating while incomes stagnate or grow at a slower pace, purchasing power declines. To compensate for the shortfall, Americans must decrease their standard of living, use their savings to fill the gap between their incomes and increasing expenditures, work longer and harder, or borrow money. None of these remedies is a desirable long-term solution; eventually, the situation will reach its limit and lead to a dead end.

However, by freezing costs, we can maintain our purchasing power. By reducing costs, we can increase our purchasing power. And by eliminating costs altogether, we can accumulate true wealth without fearing the future loss of its purchasing power. Prevailing economic concepts and policies offer no security of any kind. They are based on virtually a day-to-day existence, which certainly does not lead to a feeling of security (economic or otherwise).

2) IMPORTANT ASPECTS OF A CAREFREE ECONOMY (CAREFREEISM)

The beauty of a zero-cost economy is that once it is fully implemented, everyone will enjoy benefits unknown in modern-day America:

- We will move toward an economy powered by carefreeism.

- An economy powered by carefreeism will create general economic security while increasing our free time—a situation that few Americans can attain today.

- Economic problems that threaten or devastate many individuals and families, such as exorbitant energy costs, unemployment, inflation, and inability to afford rent, mortgage, health care, and college tuition, will fade away.

- Environmental woes will no longer plague us and our quality of life will improve.

- Carefreeism will bring economic drive in line with environmental limitations, creating a long-lasting harmony between the economy and the environment.

- As our economic woes and environmental problems start to fade, many Americans will be able to enjoy an environmentally safe prosperity.

- In a carefree economy, the rich and superrich will not have to worry about retaining their wealth. They can continue to be rich, if they so choose. The only major change will be that they will live in a peaceful economy among the rich middle-class—a much more secure situation than the one they are currently in. In other words, elite capitalists will live among general capitalists.

• Our society, which now suffocates under the burden of too little free time, will move increasingly toward a leisure society. More and more people will have more free time to travel, engage in R & D, explore new areas, and pursue similar activities. As they do so, carefreeism ultimately will produce a knowledge-based and leisure-based society. For the first time in history, all Americans will be free from economic burden and economic worries.

3) PILLARS OF A ZERO-COST, CAREFREE ECONOMY

A zero-cost, carefree economy is based on 20 main pillars, which serve as the foundation on which Florida's economy can be built. As the carefree economy progresses from infancy towards maturity, several other pillars (not discussed in this blueprint) will come into play.

No doubt, many groups and individuals will object to one or more of the pillars, claiming that implementing a zero-cost economy will infringe on their interests (though these are illusory and shortsighted). Some may take the position, "I don't care what you do to others. Just don't touch me!" Most likely, they will fail to realize that everyone in our society is being threatened by the dangerous plague of cost and everyone will benefit by eliminating it.

In fact, being among the first to help us move toward a zero-cost economy will bring benefits to the individual American. After all, no one wants to be the last person left when it comes to getting rid of the disease of plague. Likewise, we must rid ourselves of this economic plague, or at least bring it under tight control. Looking at the entire picture, everybody has plenty to gain from carefreeism.

First pillar: Use free, decentralized, environmentally safe energy sources and technologies

Without energy, nothing can happen in this world. Energy sources and energy delivery systems are enormously critical. To create a zero-cost economy and enjoy carefreeism, we must use renewable energy sources that cause no negative environmental effect and are cost-free for the consumer (once the system is paid for).

Also, energy delivery systems must be decentralized, except in densely populated areas with many high-rise buildings where space constraints preclude decentralized systems or where a decentralized system would be technologically and economically impossible. In these cases, centralized delivery systems could be used.

Cost-free (to the consumer) energy sources and decentralized energy delivery systems are extremely important for the following reasons:

- Free energy will increase the purchasing power of every Floridian and make more disposable income available. More importantly, it will trigger massive cost deceleration throughout the entire economy—the first and foremost prerequisite toward realizing a zero-cost economy and carefreeism.

- Free energy will eliminate the compounding costs associated with every increase in energy cost.

- Decentralized energy delivery systems can be made available to most households and businesses immediately. In contrast, today's centralized energy systems take at least one or two decades to produce a single British thermal unit (BTU) of energy.

- In the event of a natural or manmade catastrophe, a decentralized energy delivery system would prevent destruction and collapse of a region's entire economy, as can occur with a centralized energy system. For instance, let's say a hurricane hit Florida and destroyed a centralized energy plant, or Florida experienced a manmade emergency similar to the New York City power outage of August 2003. With a decentralized delivery system, even if tens of thousands of buildings were destroyed or the power supply systems failed, millions of others would be in full operation the very next day.

- Unlike centralized delivery systems, decentralized systems would not be subject to unknown and unforeseeable future costs.

- The social costs typically associated with an environmentally degrading centralized energy delivery system would not exist with decentralized, environmentally friendly systems.

- Decentralized systems would avoid the need to deal with wastes, such as the radioactive material of nuclear power plants. The need to eliminate wastes and protect power plants (especially nuclear plants) incurs additional financial burden and costs for centralized systems.

- Decentralized systems can promote a booming economy through decentralization of the production facilities for manufacturing the needed hardware, sales, installation, and service.

- Implementing a decentralized system would create hundreds of thousands of new jobs in this state in several different economic sectors, spread throughout Florida geographically. In contrast, with the centralized system we now have, power plants built in the future would create only 500 to 1,000 jobs—and those new jobs would be limited to the plant's vicinity. In contrast, a decentralized system would create hundreds of thousands of manufacturing and installation jobs statewide, in such fields as plumbing, roofing, and electrical wiring.

Considering these facts, the choice becomes crystal clear: We must give priority to decentralized, environmentally friendly solar delivery systems.

Second pillar: Convert existing gas-powered to electric-powered vehicles

Besides promoting the solar and wind energy industries, another effective way to create new jobs and income for many Floridians is to undertake a large-scale program to convert gas-powered vehicles to electric power (where technologically and economically possible). The same approach can be taken for the rest of the nation.

The transportation sector, dominated by personal cars, consumes more than a quarter of North America's total energy. Converting vehicles from gas to electric power would drastically reduce our dependence on imported oil. Furthermore, motor vehicles are primarily responsible for the harmful atmosphere, a significant environmental concern.

Florida has 15.7 million vehicles (8.3 million cars and 7.4 million trucks and buses). Nationwide, there are 240.9 million vehicles (136.3 million cars and 104.6 million trucks and buses). The predominant power source for these vehicles is gas—a fact we must deal with regardless of the new electric-powered cars that will be available some time after 2010. A large number of gas-powered vehicles (if not all of them) will have to be converted if they are to run on electricity, and the primary source of electricity must be solar or wind power.

Although the technology behind electric-powered vehicles is not as advanced as that of gas-powered vehicles and has not reached its maturity, it has progressed enough to be used effectively. In 1996, General Motors launched its EV1 all-electric car, which traveled 180 miles on a single charge of its nickel-metal hydride battery. Many of the 800 leaseholders loved the quiet EV1 and made overtures to GM to buy them, but were refused. In 2003, the vehicles were withdrawn and crushed. The nickel-metal hydride batteries—a tried and tested battery technology common in portable radios and other gadgets, and one that GM briefly used in the second generation of the EV1—can be easily employed to store energy for relatively long distances. A few design changes, such as integrating larger conductors within the cell would allow the batteries to deliver the tens of kilowatts needed to drive a car. They also weigh about half as much as equivalent lead-acid batteries—the type used in the first EV1s.[6]

Converting vehicles from gas to electric power would bring the following benefits:

• It would create tens of thousands of new jobs spread throughout Florida. If implemented in the rest of the country, it would create hundreds of thousands of new jobs nationwide. Considering the huge number of vehicles involved and the facilities needed to do the conversion work, clearly there's no better opportunity to create new jobs for economically depressed areas than erecting new plants (or converting existing plants) that manufacture electric motors.

6   Giles, Jim. Born to be wired. Stunning performance, awesome economy, no compromise. In: *New Scientist,* September 20, 2008, page 26 ff. Also: Brant, Bob. *Build your own electric vehicle.* McGraw-Hill/ TAB Books, New York, 1994.

- Equally important, people whose vehicles have been converted to electric power would save the money they otherwise would have had to spend on gas.

- As more vehicles are converted, the demand for gas will decrease, contributing to a drastic drop in foreign oil imports.

- The value of the U.S. dollar would start to stabilize and would be revalued compared to other major currencies, making imports cheaper.

- The budget deficit would drop, as would the interest burden on borrowed money.

- Gas prices would start to decline—good news for those who would still want to drive fast, expensive vehicles. Although this would not prove beneficial for an effective energy policy, it would give the automobile industry time to improve the performance of electric-powered cars so that fast-car enthusiasts would make the switch more willingly.

- Declining gas costs would help reduce transportation costs for foods and other goods, contributing to an overall improvement in the economic outlook.

- As the average cost of living started to drop, the cost of the reform work (such as developing alternative energy technologies and electric cars and dealing with environmental problems) also would decline.

- Manufacturers of electric motors would open a new market for export to other countries (provided we take advantage of this opportunity).

- The effects of this economic-political measure would trickle down throughout the economy, producing an economic upturn.

Thus, enforced promotion of solar and wind energy and conversion of gas-dependent to electric-powered vehicles would create a stunning economic boom whose effects would be felt all over Florida and (if implemented nationwide) the rest of the country.

Other states that provide the best conditions for converting vehicles to electric power are California, Texas, Arizona, New Mexico, and Nevada. Combined, these states have more than 72.5 million vehicles (40.3 million cars and 32.2 million trucks and buses). This huge number of vehicles could make a tremendous impact on our economy and environment, jump-starting a booming U.S. economy. Needless to say, this project would need to be implemented in conjunction with solar and wind energy programs using decentralized delivery systems.

Conversion of gas- to electric-powered vehicles, along with implementation of solar and wind energies, would be a savior to Florida and the rest of the country in both the short-term and long-term. No better or more effective measure is available, no matter how one looks at it. Without it, we cannot achieve a zero-cost economy.

Third pillar: Increase the life-span of all products

The core of capitalism rests on manufacturing products with short life spans and planned technological obsolescence. This can no longer be tolerated, because it has exacerbated the depletion of our natural resources and contributed to cost escalation—especially with regard to crude oil. Even if the earth had many more times the oil reserves than it does, the increasing cost of crude oil would create a situation akin to the near-depletion of a raw material. More importantly, with the environmental limitations caused by global warming, it's irrelevant whether greater oil reserves exist. Oil is not just an energy source but the natural source of thousands of products of all types. (Of course, the part of crude oil used as energy is of great economic and environment concern.)

If we could double a product's life span, we could immediately save 50% of the natural resources used to create that product. Using free energy to manufacture or operate products is the cornerstone of a zero-cost economy. (The next chapter will describe the economic impact of this change.)

Fourth pillar: Design products in modular form

Many industries, including the automobile and electronics industries, avoid modular designs. Why? Because it allows them to make a minor product change, yet present it as a new model the next year. There's nothing wrong with this approach when it's limited to cosmetic changes (for instance, when a carmaker changes the shape of the headlight on one of its models). In that case, it matters very little, as long as customers are willing to pay extra to get the latest model.

However, for consumers who wish to have the latest technology integrated into their vehicle (or any other product) without having to buy a new one, modular design is preferable. In modular design, the old part is simply swapped for the new one to bring that product up to date technologically, and the consumer is not forced to buy a whole new product. This capability also should be available for parts for which manufacturers make strictly cosmetic changes. In the long run, companies using modular design will discover that their products will be more popular than those lacking modular design.

Widespread use of modular design would:

- help companies win more customers
- save customers money and free up more disposable income
- allow customers to get the latest technological and cosmetic improvements without having to buy a whole new product
- cause fewer environmental problems

- conserve energy and natural resources.

Modular design is a true cost-decreasing measure and a true pillar on which a zero-cost economy can be built.

Fifth pillar: Increase productivity to the fullest extent possible

Productivity may not be everything in an economy, but without it an economy has practically nothing to count on. Thus, a permanent increase in productivity must be the primary goal of each individual, corporation, and nation seeking to enjoy a zero-cost economy to the fullest.

Why is productivity so important? Why is it a dominant factor in any economic concept, especially a zero-cost economy?

Defined simply as output per hour, productivity is the most important tool for combating cost. Productivity increases when a product is manufactured faster than it was before. The more units of a given product that are produced within a given time, the higher the manufacturer's productivity. For instance, an automobile plant normally takes 1 hour to produce a certain model; if that plant produced two models in an hour instead of one, its productivity would increase 50%.

Increasing productivity in any sector of the economy, whether manufacturing or service, would lower the average cost of goods and services. In the service sector, productivity rises when two or more services are performed in the time that a single service previously was performed. When multiple services are offered for the price of one, both the quality and productivity of the service increase. To put it another way, in the service sector increased productivity is identical to increased quality.

In the manufacturing sector, various factors typically indicate improved product quality—an increase in the product's life span, addition of new features, and a modular design. But in the service sector, increased lifespan makes no sense because it defeats the purpose of productivity. For instance, one cannot extend the service time for polishing a pair of shoes from 10 to 20 minutes, even if doing so makes the shoes shinier. In the service sector, what counts are multiple services, which not only can lower cost drastically but also increases the quality of those services. If a medical clinic were set up using this philosophy, a patient who arrived for a general check-up might undergo the following services during a single visit:

- a hormone test, which requires a saliva specimen (a 2-minute procedure)

- heavy metal testing, which entails taking a small hair specimen (a 5-minute task)

- a urine test to analyze the body's mineral and vitamin content (which involves a short walk to the restroom to urinate into a cup)

- a cholesterol test to determine cholesterol levels (which takes just a few minutes to draw blood).

Providing these multiple services at one visit would dramatically reduce the cost by increasing productivity and increasing service quality. Information resulting from these tests would be just as accurate as if the tests were split up into four different services.

This aspect of productivity and quality will play a major role in healthcare reform and cost-cutting. The next big challenge for the healthcare industry will be to implement productivity and quality in every aspect of healthcare delivery.

It will take a long time for politicians and government officials to comprehend the effectiveness of productivity and quality in the service sector, especially when it comes to healthcare costs. By now it should be clear to everyone that, despite all the rhetoric to the contrary, no U.S. administration can provide universal health care, either through government-sponsored programs or private entities, unless the cost of healthcare delivery drops drastically and is controlled through productivity and quality measures and other necessary economic-political measures (discussed later in this blueprint). The healthcare industry needs to start looking into these matters right away.

Two important issues arise with regard to a productivity increase:

- Is there a limit to the degree to which productivity can be increased?

- Is there a limit to the speed of productivity that can be reached in the manufacturing and service sectors? For example, in communications, the postal service used to be the primary means of transferring documents from one place to another. With the advent of facsimile (fax) machines, communications got much faster. Then the Internet came along, increasing communication speeds enormously; in fact, Internet speeds keep increasing nearly every day. Telephone speed-dialing is another example of an action that we can now perform much more quickly than before. In manufacturing, productivity increased greatly as factories gained the ability to change production set-ups with the push of a button. In the service sector, technology has advanced the speed at which many services can be provided; the beauty industry alone offers many examples.

A complete answer to these questions requires a more thorough analysis than is possible here. The following summary offers some guidelines.

- Manufacturing a product in a low-cost-labor country is akin to increasing productivity in a high-cost-labor country because manufacturing costs are lower (unless the latter improves productivity by using machinery). These factors help determine which area is more efficient in increasing productivity. For all practical purposes, the same rule applies to productivity increases in the service sector. Low-cost labor plus the use of machinery can increase productivity, dramatically reducing the cost of each service. Furthermore, increased productivity in the service sector can be achieved when multiple machines of the same kind are operated by fewer personnel—for instance, if one person runs multiple machines at the same time.

- Every productivity level is associated with a particular speed, which is determined by the operator's qualifications and training, development of the technology in use, and availability of the demand and delivery system. Otherwise, productivity still may lag. Consider, for instance, the technologies used to deliver the Internet, such as cable and DSL: Although Internet speeds increase all the time, the specific computer used and the operator using it must be capable of dealing with these high speeds to benefit from them. The same situation applies to other technologies used in the manufacturing and service sectors.

Thus, increasing productivity is the best way to reduce the cost of all goods and services, and represents another fast track toward attaining a zero-cost economy.

Sixth pillar: Promote a cost-efficient healthcare delivery system

No country in the world is plagued by more rapidly escalating healthcare costs than the United States. Healthcare expenditures in this country run over $2 trillion annually, or

16% of the GDP. Despite this enormous figure, more than 47 millions Americans, including 3.2 million Floridians, have no healthcare insurance. Florida has one of the highest percentages of uninsured—19%, compared to the U.S. average of 15.7%. And the quality of coverage for many Americans who *do* have healthcare insurance leaves much to be desired.

In fact, the United States has the most expensive and consequently the most inefficient healthcare system in the world. Even more worrisome is the setup of the system, which keeps costs galloping toward disaster. In light of this, two immediate questions beg answers:

- How can we make healthcare coverage available to the 3.2 million uninsured Floridians?

- How can we cut the overall cost of health care so that it is both affordable and resistant to future cost increases?

None of the existing healthcare models currently in use and none of the propositions floating around offer solutions to rising healthcare costs. The issue of cost reduction is not unique to Florida, of course; health care is a social cost that plagues the entire country. Unless we reduce it drastically and immediately, the specific type of healthcare delivery system we have—nationalized or private—is irrelevant.

To attain a carefree economy, healthcare costs must be reduced or eliminated because they lead to unnecessary social costs. If such costs keep rising unchallenged, even the best healthcare delivery system will not last long and eventually will collapse. Floridians would be a big step closer toward achieving a zero-cost economy if we had no healthcare costs. Unfortunately, this will never happen (even if medical science could control all diseases) simply because there will always be events that incur healthcare costs, such as accidents and injuries.

To combat rising healthcare costs in Florida, a series of sound economic and political decisions must be made. Furthermore, an efficient and productivity-oriented delivery system based on semi-homogenous multispecialty clinic (SHMSC) facilities must be strongly promoted.[7] This goal could be easily pursued through tax incentives, which would go into effect after the project is completed. To reach this goal, further incentives could be offered through low or even zero-interest rate loans and similar measures.

Other significant measures also must be implemented to make the healthcare delivery system cost efficient. These include the following:

- Standardize fees for all medical services, whether paid by insurance companies or individuals. (*Note:* Often different fees are charged for the same services, depending on the payer.)

- Introduce flat rates for physician, clinic, emergency, and hospital visits and services.

- Simplify accounting and payment systems between the insurance companies and service providers.

- Give healthcare providers a free hand in deciding which tests and treatments a patient needs, based on the level of knowledge, facilities, and equipment available in that area. This would help reduce the fear of malpractice lawsuits resulting from failure to perform certain scans, cardiac catheterization, or other expensive tests.

- Revoke the medical licenses of physicians who commit three medical malpractices in a 1-year period.

- Reform the tort system in favor of victims.

---

7   Khavari, Farid A. Productivity-Inducing Competition (PIC), The Key to Universal and Affordable Quality Health Care. In: *Carefreeism,* ibid.

Farid A. Khavari, PhD

- Combat fraud in every possible way by setting high licensing standards, and increase the punishment to discourage such behavior, especially with regard to Medicare fraud (a flourishing enterprise in Miami.)

- Impose monetary incentives and punishments with regard to insurance premiums, to either encourage or discourage certain behaviors. We should promote fewer doctor visits and discourage doctors from having patients visit their clinics frequently without good reason. Also, we should encourage medical testing to prevent an illness from becoming more serious and more expensive. Along the same lines, we should urge people to exercise more, use alternative therapies when appropriate, change unhealthy lifestyles and behaviors (such as violence and drunk driving), and alter modifiable risk factors for disease (such as obesity). These steps should help the entire healthcare system move in the right direction.[8]

- Stop the pharmaceutical industry's attempt to make Americans increasingly dependent on drugs. (Their attempt brings to mind the enforced sale of opium to the Chinese by British merchants to pay for goods in great demand in the West, such as porcelain, silk, and tea.) Further proof of this attempt is the erecting of CVS and Walgreens stores in staggering numbers nationwide; no other types of stores are being built in such close vicinity to one another.

In short, we must look at healthcare costs as social costs and make serious efforts to reduce them drastically. Only then can

---

8   Khavari, Farid A. *Vultures - Doctors, Lawyers, Hospitals and the Insurance Companies, What's Wrong, and What to Do About It.* Roundtable Pub., 1991. (This book reflects the author's experience with medical malpractice lawsuits in Miami after his late wife was killed in 1978. He spent the next 2 years participating in every deposition and observing the entire process.)

we have a decent, well-functioning healthcare delivery system, in turn allowing us to have a zero-cost economy.

Seventh pillar: Promote building ownership for small businesses

Small businesses provide about 70% of the jobs overall and create 90% of new jobs in the United States. This fact alone demands that we pay special attention to small businesses. Every economic-political measure we implement should promote these businesses and more importantly, cut their operational costs slowly but surely. This would bring Florida one step closer to a zero-cost economy.

We should implement all measures to help start-up companies develop new technologies and products and make efforts to increase productivity in the manufacturing and service sectors. As discussed earlier, increased productivity in the service sector corresponds to an increase in quality[9].

Furthermore, we should make low-interest or zero-interest financing available to key small businesses to help them grow and fulfill rising demands, in terms of jobs and products. Also, we should help small businesses cut recurring costs—primarily rent and energy. This will stabilize the cost of their products or services. Like interest, energy and rent not only increase the cost of products and services but also compound as well. The first pillar (above) addressed the importance of free energy. As for rent, typically this rises annually, as do property taxes paid by the tenant. Unless small business owners are freed from this financial burden, they will either lose customers due to the need to increase their prices or will go out of business if they cannot transfer increased costs to customers. As a result,

---

9   Khavari, Farid A. Productivity-Inducing Competition (PIC), The Key to Universal and Affordable Quality Health Care. In: *Carefreeism,* ibid.

costs will rise or the base of job creation in Florida will start to disappear—and we will fail to create a zero-cost economy.

To avert this situation, we must help small businesses buy their properties free and clear so they can eliminate recurring costs and consequently stabilize their prices. This will move the entire economy in the direction of cost reduction—a big step toward a zero-cost economy.

Eighth pillar: Use tax incentives to develop and manufacture environmentally safe and friendly new technologies

Practically speaking, the core of a capitalist economic system is based on availability of free energy and raw materials. In the past, Britain, the Netherlands, and other nations colonized Third World countries to exploit their raw materials. More recently, the United States invaded oil-rich Iraq in the hope of controlling its oil supply.

Capitalism can survive only if production costs (labor, energy, and raw materials) are low. In reality, other costs, such as the cost of environmental destruction and technological development, must be added to production costs. For this reason, many American companies have been outsourcing manufacturing to low-cost-labor countries. The escalating cost of energy and natural resources on the one hand and environmental limitations (primarily global warming) on the other hand have thrown the capitalist system off balance.

Although cost is the biggest enemy of capitalism, no one has tried to reduce cost on the demand side. All that mattered was to reduce production costs. As long as the cost increase could be transferred to consumers, the system could continue as it was. But times are changing rapidly and dramatically, especially with the drastic rise in crude oil prices and consequently in the prices of other goods and services. For the first time, capitalism faces a serious problem.

Also, capitalism has largely shunned innovation and R & D because these activities increase cost. So as capitalist countries outsource the production of goods to low-cost-labor countries, they also transfer innovation and R & D to those countries. Granted, many large corporations that outsource have maximized their profits, but only in the short term. As the realization takes hold that free energy is a necessity, the manufacturing base is fading, and the economy is in disarray. Yet new technologies must be developed and manufacturing plants must be built.

The solution is clear: Speed the development of environmentally safe, alternative, renewable energy sources. This would give us immediate access to cheap or free energy. To achieve this goal would require immediate action and initial capital. To encourage the influx of private investors, the government should provide tax incentives to make the needed projects launch quickly and attain great success.

The problem with tax incentives is that no one has figured out how to implement them effectively. The supply-side school of economics believes that giving tax cuts to the rich stimulates the economy. This theory is entirely wrong. Rich people do not invest because they have received tax cuts. They invest because of the profit-maximizing drive. When an opportunity arises, they borrow capital, if necessary to maximize profit. Tax cuts alone would not encourage them if we implement them as we have in the past.

This blueprint proposes a new way of implementing tax incentives. Let's assume the government wants to promote development of alternative energy technologies with certain specifications and requirements. To achieve this goal, it should announce that all companies that develop these technologies will be tax exempt for the next 20 years (just to use an example). The effective date of the tax exemption would be the date when the company introduces the eligible products on the market. Offering a sales tax exemption to people who buy these products would enhance the incentive. To further stimulate investment and development, the government could provide tax write-offs to shareholders of these companies and make dividends and capital gains tax exempt for shareholders.

These measures would reap the following benefits:

- The government would obtain new technologies without spending a penny, reaching a goal that previously would have been possible only with massive government spending.

- Although the government would not collect tax revenues from the involved companies for the designated period, the effect would be neutral from the standpoint of tax revenues because no revenues were generated before the technology was developed. Also, the multiplicative effects of the new technologies would create an economic boom that would bring massive tax revenues.

- The relationship between the government and these companies would become more productive and result-oriented.

- These companies would become interested in developing long-term projects. Say, for instance, the original technology a company developed became obsolete within the designated 20-year period, leading to sales declines and loss of tax exemptions. In this case, the company would want to be able to benefit from the earned tax exemption at least for that period, so it would strive to improve the technology. Thus, a long-term goal would become a reality. (Currently, the profit-maximizing drive means virtually no U.S. companies have long-term goals; this is a key cause of our economic downturn and increasing economic problems.)

Implementing tax incentives as just described would not reward corporations and investors just because they are rich nor would it give them preferential tax treatment. Instead, it would force corporations and investors to *earn* tax incentives. For a tax incentive to work properly, it must be awarded on the basis of performance, not favoritism. The tax cuts currently offered by politicians and recommended by economists are totally misguided and will fail to realize the desired goals. Tax incentives must be used to develop technologies that help implement a zero-cost economy.

Ninth pillar: Keep interest rates low and bring sanity in regard to interest

Of the two unpopular concepts, taxes and interest, interest is worse. We pay taxes when we make a financial gain of some type, as from a salary, dividends, or an inheritance. In contrast, a person pays interest because he or she has no money (or not enough money) and has to borrow.

Interest has an additional negative effect: Unlike taxes, it compounds. Interest is an evil for any borrower, whether an individual, a business, or a government. All borrowers must pay heftily for the money they borrow or owe. Nothing is worse for an economy than extortionate interest rates, such as those imposed by credit card companies and subprime lenders. (Taxes, in contrast, are immune from this threat.)

Interest is a plague on any economy. It must be reduced to zero or at least minimized to the extent possible. Why doesn't a single politician talk about the wickedness of interest, especially the effect of high interest rates on the economic well-being of our citizens and government? Instead, everyone lambastes taxes. In absolute terms, rich people have to pay a large amount of taxes. Tax cuts would leave them with more money; they can make even more money by lending money and reaping the interest if other alternatives are not attractive enough. For anyone on the receiving end, interest is welcome because it brings more money.

Of course, the opposite is true for those who borrow money and must pay interest. The rich gain from high interest rates, whereas the poor and middle class suffer—a primary reason why we must keep interest rates under control.

The Federal Reserve Bank (known as the Fed) uses interest rates to influence the relationship between full employment and low inflation in favor of one or another, depending on the prevailing state of the economy. In practical terms though, these are contradictory goals. Thus, this policy has its limits and cannot be implemented successfully, as has been proven time and time again. For instance, if productivity (a cost-dampening measure) increases faster than the inflation rate, inflation is not likely to increase; in fact, it would decline. This is the shortcoming of what is known as the Phillips curve, which represents the inverse relationship between the inflation rate and the unemployment rate. This concept is the foundation of the Fed's failed policy.

In its present authority, the Fed tries to influence the outcome of inflation and unemployment in the desired direction by using discount policy of increasing or decreasing interest rates depending on prevailing economic conditions to achieve the set goal. This is a primitive measure fraught with limitations. In fact, it makes the Fed's existence practically unnecessary.

The Fed's first and foremost duty should be to provide money to those industry sectors that make our economy float and function properly. To achieve this goal, it must make zero-interest-rate funds available to sectors that merit full attention, such as those involved in manufacturing alternative energy technologies and vehicles powered by solar or wind energy. The Fed should avoid supporting industries that have been riddled with "bubbles" and scams, such as real estate, construction, and others based on speculation. In other words, an *expansive* monetary policy should be used for critical industry sectors such as energy and transportation whereas a *contractive* monetary policy is needed for sectors such as real estate and construction.

Assuming the Fed would approve such a policy, the outcome would be to promote the manufacturing of alternative energy and solar- and electric-powered vehicles, thus creating jobs virtually overnight and stimulating the economy. This would vastly decrease our dependence on foreign crude oil and greatly reduce the flow of dollars to unfriendly countries. More Americans would earn incomes and start buying real estate and our economy would grow more robust.

The recent collapse of the real estate market stemmed largely from scams by dishonest lenders who used deceptive subprime loans to dupe people into using their savings, equities, and livelihood to buy real estate at artificially set prices. These lenders lured innocent and financially uneducated people who hoped to make money and become rich. Unfortunately, most of these borrowers experienced financial disaster while a few got rich. The government also has fallen victim to this situation after first getting hefty property taxes. As we know, the subprime scam has contributed heavily to budget deficits, rising unemployment, downsizing, and a shattered economy.

Therefore, the foundation of a healthy zero-cost economy is to eliminate interest rates. (For details, see Chapter 4, Part 5: Making the Federal Reserve Bank effective and purposeful.) If we let interest rates run amok, we will have to pay hefty interest on every slice of pizza or piece of chicken we eat. As it is, we are well on our way toward this scenario, with many Americans using credit cards to pay for meals, taking refuge in whatever line of credit they still have. We must stop this disastrous trend before it destroys our economy.

We must also reform our credit-reporting system, which is based on exploiting consumers and favoring financial institutions. Credit-reporting agencies use a credit rating system in which people with lower credit scores have to pay higher interest rates. It's absurd to think such people will become more financially responsible by having to pay higher interest rates. Higher rates only make them poorer and ultimately create a backlash for financial institutions. In fact, this punitive system creates more problems of all kinds, causing people to take refuge in negative, irrational behaviors.

In addition, we must improve our credit-scoring system. Before a bank or other company can post a negative report on a consumer, a copy of that report should be sent to the consumer for a response and that response should be posted.

In short, we must outlaw high interest rates, subprime loans, and other extortionate interest practices that pose a threat to our economy and prevent us from attaining a zero-cost economy. Interest in any form is the biggest hindrance to realizing and maintaining a zero-cost economy. In the long term, it must disappear.

Tenth pillar: Make home ownership fast and easy for every Floridian

For most of us, the home is a sacred place where the family lives together. The home sets the foundation of love, staying together, and cooperation among family members—the very foundation of society.

The goal of any government should be to set conditions that allow every family to own a home and live in it peacefully and with dignity. Instead, when a home becomes an insecure place, the family becomes insecure, creating problems that only increase the social costs to society.

Furthermore, a home must be a place where the family *lives*—not an object for speculation. No one speculates with a spouse and children; a home must be regarded the same way. People should not use their home equity to speculate in real estate and take the chance of losing their present home, as has happened all too often in recent years.

In a zero-cost economy, a home not only would be available to every family, but buying a home would be easy and fast. To achieve this goal, we must create the following conditions:

- Eliminate real estate speculation of all types.

- Keep home prices relatively low.

- Prevent arbitrary price increases to decrease the incentive to speculate.

- Drastically revise property taxes so they are fair and free from the effect of artificially inflated real estate prices. (Remember—every hike in real estate values is associated with a hike in property taxes. It's an open question whether lower real estate values and low property taxes are more advantageous in the long run than drastically increased real estate values and rising property taxes, considering that most people intend to live in their homes for a long time. If property taxes keep rising uncontrolled or uncontrollably, no one will be able to afford to stay in their homes when their incomes start to shrink because the increased property taxes will be unaffordable. As property taxes tend to increase over time while incomes tend to decline, this situation cannot serve homeowners for long, especially when a property's value drops below the amount the homeowner owes on it. In this situation, many people simply give up on their homes and the banks sit on properties that continue to lose value.)

- Keep interest rates on mortgages low—no more than 2% to 3%. At best, eliminate them altogether.

- Use every imaginable financing method to reduce the life of a mortgage so it does not exceed 15 years (or, preferably, 10 years).

- Eliminate all penalties for paying off a mortgage early.

These rules should apply to all families willing to own one home and live there; purchase of additional homes for speculation and as a source of income (that is, rental properties) should be excluded from these conditions. In fact, the opposites of those points should apply for homes purchased for speculation or income generation.

Implementing these policies would be a huge stride toward realizing a zero-cost economy. Families would end up owning their homes free and clear in a relatively short time. The home would provide family members of all ages a place to live with dignity. Seniors would not have to worry about where they will live, especially at a time when they are less capable of taking care of themselves and typically have less money.

What about homeowners who wish to upgrade their homes to more expensive ones? In this case, the conditions detailed above would apply, with the restriction that the previous home must be sold or be subject to the same terms that apply to speculative and income-generating properties (unless the owners give or sell that home to one of their children who is married and raising a family).

In all likelihood, some people would try to take advantage of this system. This risk will exist until economic security is established completely. Once we achieve a zero-cost economy, multiple home ownership will be more of a headache than a source of financial gain. Few people will give up a peaceful and economically secure life for the worries and financial burdens of owning multiple homes with no obvious advantage.

Easing home ownership not only would reduce the burden of major mortgage payments and provide a secure place for family and retirement. It also would eliminate speculation. Building homes for speculative purposes (as has occurred in Miami and elsewhere in the United States) has incurred steep social costs, such as increased unemployment, foreclosures, bankruptcies, deficits, environmental destruction, exploitation of natural resources, and—to put it bluntly—looming devastation for mankind. We simply cannot keep making this mistake.

Eleventh pillar: Ensure a general free education

A nation's most valuable treasure is its educated citizens. The higher the level of the citizenry's education and the greater the number of educated people (in terms of percentage as well as absolute figures), the easier it will be to implement positive changes.

After all, the education of American scientists made it possible to land mankind on the moon. In fact, the Apollo spacecraft had fewer electronic components than today's Corvette. Looking back, it seems amazing that we sent a man to the moon. Our amazement reflects the declining level of Americans' education. The Apollo space program was possible largely because during the 1960s and 1970s, we had plenty of engineers to work on the projects that made this country great. And Florida participated in a huge share of that endeavor.

Today, though, many young people study financing and aspire to become mortgage brokers so they can make fast money—an occupation that does not bring a secure future for themselves or the nation. It is high time that education, the right kind of education, take a front seat. To achieve this goal, we need to take the following steps:

- Make education cost-free from kindergarten all the way through college and beyond.[10] We should encourage students to graduate in multiple disciplines so they can expand their horizons and resolve problems better.

- Put teachers' incomes on a par with those of other well-paid professionals. This would relieve them of financial worries so they could concentrate on delivering high-quality education.

- Create rewards and prizes for outstanding accomplishments and achievements by both teachers and students.

- Pay special attention to subjects critical to mankind's future and to improving our economy, environment, and health (such as energy, health care, and environmental science).

---

10 The author is an example of someone who received a free education from kindergarten through the doctorate level. If a country such as Germany (where the author received his PhD) can offer free higher education to foreign students, surely a great nation such as the United States can do the same. In Germany, education was free until recently; unfortunately, that country has taken a step backward by transferring much of the cost of education to students.

- Elevate the quality of the average level of education in the United States to the top three nations in the world, if not the very top of the scale.

- Provide both males and females with the highest level of education with added focus on educating females because they will be the mothers of the next generation.

Knowledge and education must become as free and as freely available as air and water. There is no other sound way for a nation to achieve greatness. To do this, we must give teachers hefty financial rewards because they educate our next generation. In short, education must be at the top of our political and economic agenda. A dramatically improved educational system and a greater educational level for all Americans will make it easier for everyone to understand and attain a zero-cost economy. As our educational level improves, Americans will also enjoy other gains, both individually and as a nation.

Twelfth pillar: Promote ethical profit making and reduce the profit-maximizing drive

Nobody would deny that profit-making is the motivation behind any business. Nor would anyone question that businesses should make a profit. A company that does not make a profit will not last long.

However, when a company is driven solely by the goal of maximizing profit, serious ethical questions arise. Undue emphasis on maximizing profit can lead to devastating costs and in the long run, failure of that company. Profit-maximizing drive can cause people to use the following unethical tactics:

- deceptive sales practices and advertising

- dishonesty with customers

- lying on reports or falsifying records

- treating employees and customers unfairly
- practicing discrimination of all types
- making bribes and kickbacks
- charging for undelivered goods and services
- threatening consumers with negative credit reporting to extract money from them
- inflating invoices to increase business (but in the meantime souring customer relations)
- using low credit scores to extract more money from financially distressed customers, hurting them even more
- using excuses to extract unjustified money from customers. (Credit-card companies use profit maximizing to justify charging late fees for a late payment, even when the borrowed money carries an interest rate above 20%. Those customers may be doomed to paying interest on the borrowed money forever.)

These practices not only are unethical, unfair, wrong, and shortsighted from the standpoint of keeping long-term customers; they also create tremendous social costs which we cannot and should not tolerate. Unfortunately, these practices are so deep-rooted in the economy of Florida and the United States that it's almost a surprise when we encounter honest businesses. Equally perplexing, government agencies increasingly are being driven by the same unethical profit-maximizing drive. For example, they allow real estate prices to keep rising through speculation and subprime mortgage manipulations because that enables them to collect more property taxes.

Another example is how some Florida municipalities issue traffic tickets. For instance, a motorist received a $75 citation for having dark-tinted car windows. Although he paid the fine in a timely manner, he received another notice for $91 that demanded $16 more (after deducting the $75 fine). These and similar revenue-generating tactics are both unethical and shortsighted. No doubt, after a few bad experiences, more and more drivers eventually will start resisting them. Even worse, people will avoid the areas where such practices occur, causing the economy of those areas to suffer. This effect will outweigh the revenue generated by the profit-maximizing drive. A much wiser approach would be to promote ethical behavior in conjunction with a friendlier and more sound policy.

Are ethics, quality, and profit compatible? At first sight, especially considering the tactics just mentioned, the answer would seem to be no. But in a zero-cost economy, these three principles would be harmonious. Using ethical means to maximize profit would eliminate unnecessary cost while bringing greater and more long-term profit to businesses. In turn, these businesses would increasingly gain customers' trust.

Equally important is creating long-term goals for businesses in the form of tax incentives, as discussed earlier. This would encourage executives to distance themselves from short-term profit maximizing. Having long-terms goals is likely to lead them away from unethical practices and the profit-maximizing drive altogether. To achieve this objective, we must promote ethical corporate behavior; where this is not possible, we must enact new regulations. The bottom line: To create a zero-cost economy, we need to reduce and ultimately eliminate unethical corporate behavior.

Thirteenth pillar: Limit lobbyists' influence

Proponents of the capitalist economic system in the United States boast that its operation is based on a free-market economy. They claim our economic woes will resolve and an equilibrium will be reached through the interplay of free-market forces—meaning that the price corrects the level of demand.

In theory, this may be true. And this concept also may apply from the microeconomic standpoint. However, with thorough scrutiny, it's clear that free-market forces play practically no macroeconomic role. Instead, the elite capitalists call all the shots. For instance, the elite capitalists:

- support politicians who are friendly to their interests by making massive contributions to their campaigns (both directly and indirectly)
- influence politicians through lobbyists on their payrolls
- advertise for or against politicians who are for or against their interests.

These tactics run counter to a fair political climate that serves and protects the general public's interests. However, eliminating them will be difficult. Advertising cannot be outlawed due to freedom of speech. Nonetheless, lobbyists must be barred from having direct access to politicians and from giving money to them, either directly to an individual politician or collectively to the political party that supports a particular candidate.

Allowing lobbyists to influence politicians imposes tremendous costs and prevents economic and technological progress. It also contributes to environmental problems and the depletion of natural resources (in itself a cost-escalating factor). Even worse, correcting this problem becomes tremendously more costly as time passes, causing greater economic suffering for many Americans.

Just look at the sorry case of U.S. automakers. Had their lobbyists not influenced Congress to pass legislation protecting them with regard to gas mileage and made short-term profit maximizing possible, they would not be suffering as much as they currently are. Such legislation contributed to a rise in crude oil prices and environmental devastation. Many more examples of other industry lobbying exist, but discussing these would lead us away from the main subject.

All parties—individuals as well as industries and corporations—should be able to access their legislators to convey their concerns and suggestions and to ask for help. Wallet size should not determine who gets more attention. Why should large corporations and elite capitalists get preferential attention simply because of their financial strength? For the sake of economic and social justice, members of the general public need to be able to communicate easily with their legislative representatives.

To reiterate a crucial point, we must discourage and eliminate cost-generating actions in the interest of creating a zero-cost economy. Lobbyists' influence in shaping U.S. or Florida policy must be eliminated for good, as it takes a tremendous toll on our economy and environment.

Fourteenth pillar: Give tax incentives or exemptions to companies and investors for developing solar and wind energy technologies

The common perception is that multinational corporations are villains that exploit natural resources, despoil the environment, and outsource work in the interest of maximizing profit—in short, these multinational corporations care only for their own well-being. In most cases, these stereotypes are true. But hurting or destroying such corporations by levying taxes on them would not help resolve our problems. In fact, it would only compound them because we would be destroying a crucial source of expertise and technology.

It is equally shortsighted and absurd for local or state governments to offer billions of dollars to lure foreign companies with obsolete technologies to set up plants in their localities when they could spend far less to create new jobs and high-tech manufacturing plants for alternative energy technologies and sources.[11] Tax incentives also could boost the financial requirements and profits of companies with appropriate technological concepts (along with their investors), eliminating the "fat cats" of Wall Street and elsewhere who prey on those looking to invest their hard-earned savings and make financial gains.

To tap into the resources of these and other companies striving to develop much-needed technologies, we should provide tax incentives of all kinds, as described earlier. As long as money makes companies do the right things and the public reaps the benefits, a responsible government with foresight should do everything possible to encourage them.

---

11   Milne, Richard: U.S. becomes the low-cost site of the moment for manufacturers. In: *Financial Times,* London, England, September 8, 2008, p. 1. (According to this article, the state of Tennessee "… has disclosed that it agreed to give German carmaker Volkswagen $577 million in incentives for its $1 billion plant in Chattanooga". The article notes that "ThyssenKrupp, the German steelmaker and industrial group, is receiving more than $811 million to build a new steel mill in Alabama. It turned down even more from Louisiana, which reportedly offered as much as $2 billion, as well as an additional $900 million in cheap debt from Alabama, which it declined as it wished to remain debt-free." Why can't we spend this money for local or national entrepreneurs to develop and manufacture solar and wind energy technologies or to set up factories that manufacture electric motors to power existing vehicles as well as provide incentives to build facilities that convert vehicles to electrical power? Has anyone considered these and similar possibilities, which would create more jobs than the low-cost sites would? The latter sites would become like Third World manufacturing plants for foreign companies with obsolete technology. What's more, providing facilities to improve the obsolete technologies would be done at our expense. It's high time we thought smart and took a long-term view.)

Income tax incentives are an issue for the federal government. Little can be done at the state level. Nonetheless, an enthusiastic and economically minded Florida governor acting in concert with other governors could promote a policy of appropriate income tax incentives by influencing the federal government.

Fifteenth pillar: Introduce the "green tax"

"Greening" of the economy in every possible way is the steppingstone to a zero-cost economy. Besides making our economy more sustainable, it would make our lives more livable. Although many companies have chosen to go green, many more are still governed by the profit-maximizing drive (even if they claim to be concerned about the environment). To speed our progress toward a zero-cost economy and reduce the profit-maximizing drive in favor of ethical profit, we must introduce the "green tax," which would apply only to technological products.

Before going into more detail, I would like to point out that some people believe anything with the word "tax" in it is bad. However, the "green tax" can help deter environmentally damaging activities while encouraging and boosting sales of environmentally sound technologies and products. We could achieve similar results by implementing the "health tax" (the sixteenth pillar, discussed below), whose purpose is to deter sales of health-damaging foods and encourage health-inducing activities.

The "green tax" would apply only to products that *do not* meet these three requirements:

- technological products that carry at least a 10-year warranty in life span and ability to function

- products whose modular design allows integration of advances into the design of the existing product

- products with independent power-generating features and technology that are powered by "green" energy.

To encourage companies to meet these requirements, we should exempt the qualifying products from sales tax, depending on how important the product is for the economy in general and for consumers in particular. Examples of products that would fall into this category include decentralized solar energy systems and electric vehicles powered by solar or wind energy. A state agency could be created to endorse such products. Official labels would indicate that the product fulfills the requirements and is exempt from the green tax. With this small step that uses both the stick and the carrot, we would be taking a large leap toward a zero-cost economy.

Sixteenth pillar: Introduce the "health tax"

According to the *American Journal of Health Promotion*, each obese employee costs a company 56% more in health insurance than a normal-weight employee. Besides increasing healthcare costs, obesity and certain other health conditions incur high social costs, resulting in more doctors' visits, medical treatments, emergency health care, surgery, and other expenditures. Of course, healing disease should remain the top priority of healthcare providers, but we need to move toward preventive health care to bring costs down and control them at a very low level.

The first significant step would be to change Americans' eating habits and make healthier foods available at more grocery stores and restaurants. (After all, one needs to be healthy to enjoy the benefits of a zero-cost economy.) Introducing a "health tax" would help us reach this goal. As with the "green tax," some people might take offense to this proposal simply because it is called a tax. But they should realize that just as tax incentives encourage good behaviors, taxation discourages bad behaviors. Eating the wrong foods and eating too much are bad habits that cause health problems—and these behaviors must be discouraged because they incur enormous healthcare costs, social costs of all kind, and premature death.

However, before punishing people for their bad habits and punishing stores and restaurants for selling unhealthy foods, we must give them plenty of advance notice before putting the "health tax" into effect. This would give them a chance to change their ways.

The "health tax" should help move the healthcare system toward preventive medicine, promoting healthier, safer, and less expensive care than the largely "curative" medicine practiced today. This tax should apply to:

- foods not grown naturally (this would make unhealthy foods more expensive and encourage people to make healthier choices)

- supersized portions of fast foods, such as hamburgers and sodas (supersized foods create supersized people)

- foods prepared with harmful and unhealthy ingredients, such as saturated fats.

The altered eating habits achieved through a "health tax" would help reduce certain illnesses, especially obesity, hearth attacks, strokes, and cancer. The result would be a drastic reduction in healthcare costs.

Seventeenth pillar: Promote the agricultural superfoods industry

Increasing food costs could soon lead to another crisis—one that will increase poverty and frustration. The situation is getting worse as more and more agricultural land and products are used to produce ethanol. Rising demand for food from countries with emerging economies only compounds the problem.

For any government, a large task in the future will be to fill the stomachs of its people with diets that contain the right blend of micronutrients. Making nutrition-rich foods (called superfoods) available can decrease healthcare costs tremendously. Deficiencies in vitamins, minerals, and other nutrients can cause many health problems. According to the World Health Organization, almost 1 billion people worldwide suffer from goiter, a neck swelling brought on by an enlarged thyroid gland related to lack of dietary iodine. Iodine deficiency also leads to measurable brain damage in almost 50 million people and causes cretinism (a stunted growth condition) in another 16 million.[12] Although people can avoid nutritional deficiencies by taking vitamin and mineral supplements, eating superfoods instead may be preferable.

Unfortunately, it is virtually impossible to grow naturally micronutrient-rich crops in nutritionally depleted land. Using genetic engineering to boost a crop's nutrient content is questionable, unless the land is fortified with natural and rich fertilizers (animal manure). Florida's climate provides ideal conditions for all types of fruits, vegetables, and many other crops. We must develop the capability of growing foods naturally rich in nutrients, instead of fortifying them with those the body does not absorb well.

Promoting healthy, nutrition-rich foods is another cornerstone of a zero-cost economy. Good nutrition can help reduce healthcare costs and improve health. The economy would benefit as well from creation of this new industry and the new jobs it would create.

---

12   Walker, Matt. Superfoods wanted. In: *New Scientist,* London, September 13, 2008.

Eighteenth pillar: Balance the budget

A balanced budget indicates that an economy is being operated within its means and financial capability. A budget surplus indicates the economy is performing well, creating more income than cost. Conversely, a budget deficit signals that the economy is doing poorly or is being poorly run.

No entity—whether a household, a private company, or a local, state, or federal government—can last long with a continuous budget deficit. An economy whose foundation rests on speculation, especially in real estate, is likely to suffer from budget deficits during an economic downturn. The government cannot collect adequate tax revenues to cover expenses when many properties are being foreclosed and people start losing their jobs. Contraction of the economy not only decreases tax revenues but also compounds the problem, leading to even lower tax revenues as companies cut jobs to save money.

To compensate for lower tax revenues, governments often use such primitive and noninnovative measures as raising taxes, cutting services and jobs, dipping into reserves, borrowing money, and leasing or selling assets. One need not be clairvoyant to see the limitations of these measures; eventually, the government will run out of options.

The most prudent way for a government to prevent a budget deficit is to implement the principles of a zero-cost economy. Like private households that strive towards zero-cost living, governments must follow the principles of a zero-cost economy. Every household that moves towards zero cost requires a lower income—much less an income with annually increasing percentage rates to maintain its purchasing power. Balancing a budget is a matter of maintaining purchasing power for the goods and services a household uses. A deficit occurs when purchasing power declines.

Farid A. Khavari, PhD

Once a budget deficit exists, we should avoid conventional methods such as raising taxes, cutting programs and jobs, dipping into reserves, borrowing money, and leasing or selling assets to finance failed and bloated programs that only compound and prolong our economic distress. The right approach is to promote technologies and products that contribute to creating a zero-cost economy on the one hand and increase productivity on the other hand—which is a total antideficit strategy and policy.

Nineteenth pillar: Build wealth in real terms for everyone's retirement

Following the principles of a zero-cost economy is the only known way to build wealth with 100% security. Remember—if costs aren't frozen, reduced, or eliminated, they will always exist and will keep escalating and accelerating until they eventually exceed income. No matter how high a person's salary or other income, it's only a matter of time before accumulated wealth melts away like a block of ice in the desert. The faster the rate at which costs increase, the faster one's wealth dwindles. Wealth can match escalating and accelerating costs only when income and wealth grow at least at the same pace as costs. However, this is not always the case, so few people have the privilege of enjoying this situation.

One must not assume that Social Security income, saving accounts, stock holdings, certificates of deposit (CDs), money market accounts, currency speculation, real estate, or running a successful business alone will guarantee wealth building if general costs are not frozen, reduced, and finally eliminated (if possible). Once zero-cost living for individual households becomes possible or a zero-cost economy is created, all of these sources can provide added income. However, their speculative aspects must be eliminated in the interest of ensuring a stable economy and a peaceful, financially secure retirement.

Keep in mind the three important foundations of a zero-cost economy:

- If general costs are frozen, the purchasing power of a stagnating income is maintained.

- If general costs are reduced, the purchasing power of a stagnating income increases and the person can save toward building wealth.

- If general costs are totally eliminated, the purchasing power of a stagnating income becomes a total savings and will help build true wealth.

Once any of these conditions occurs, income derived from nonspeculative sources (such as Social Security, pensions, or CDs) that do not carry fees or other charges can add to wealth in the full amount, minus taxes that may be levied on such income. Conversely, speculative investments, such as those made in the stock market, money-market accounts, currencies, real estate, and businesses, can increase wealth if they succeed, but will decrease or even destroy wealth if they fail. Thus, it's clear that a zero-cost economy is the best path to a financially secure retirement.

Twentieth pillar: Reduce income inequality

One of the most pressing issues for both the United States and Florida is the growing income inequality between the rich and the middle class. To put it simply, the rich are getting richer while the middle class gets poorer.

Proponents of income inequality (most of whom are conservatives) offer a host of reasons to justify the growing income disparity. The conservatives' strongest argument is that incomes are unequal because the top income earners work more and are better educated.[13] They emphasize that the top fifth of wage earners perform one-third of all labor in the U.S. economy; in contrast, most wage earners in the bottom fifth do not work at all.[14] They remind us it is unjust to take from one person and give to another to equalize wealth. Justice demands equal opportunities, they contend, not equal incomes.[15]

Liberals counter that income leveling is not just about raising lower incomes but also about pulling higher incomes down. Today, the mega-rich make obscene amounts of money. In 1975, General Electric's CEO made 36 times the average family income ($500,000); in 2000, the same corporation's then-CEO, Jack Welch, pulled in 3,500 times the average family income ($144.5 million).[16] In addition, incomes at the top are rising faster than those at the bottom. The majority of the income increases for the bottom half of the wage distribution comes from workers taking second jobs and working more, not from pay increases.[17]

Whatever the reasoning of both sides, if one traces income inequality to its roots, one sees that it stems from factors other than hard work, higher education, and the like. Income

---

13   Rector, Robert and Hederman, Jr., Rea S. Two Americas: One Rich, One Poor? Understanding Income Inequality in the United States. The Heritage Foundation, August 8, 2004.

14   Ibid.

15   Kellard, Joseph. Don't narrow my gap! Why narrowing "income gaps" is unjust. *Capitalism Magazine,* February 28, 2004; Walberg, Herbert and Bast, Joseph L. *Education and Capitalism: How Overcoming Our Fear of Markets and Economics Can Improve America's Schools,* Chapter 6. Hoover Institution Press, 2003; Machan, Tibor R. The errors of egalitarianism; in: Tibor R. Machan (ed.), *Liberty and Equality.* Hoover Institution Press, 2002.

16   Pizzigati, Sam. The rich and the rest. In: *The Futurist,* July/August 2005, p. 40; Krugman, Paul. Faltering meritocracy in America. In: *The Economist,* London. January 1, 2005.

17   Leonardt, David: Time to slay the inequality myth? Not so fast. In: *New York Times,* January 25, 2004.

inequality stems from nothing but the drive for personal income-maximizing in the interest of living the lavish lifestyle of the rich and famous. Of course, other drives, such as the drive for maximizing power and control, also come into play.

The argument that someone who is intelligent, knowledgeable, educated, and hard working is worth 3,500 more than anyone else in the world is absurd. No one can be 3,500 times smarter than the world's dumbest person can. Similarly, no hard-working person works 3,500 times harder than the laziest person on earth. There are millions of smarter, better-educated, and harder-working people than the brightest and highest-earning CEOs in corporate America—and these millions of people earn no more than a middle-class person does. A musician who spends 16 hours a day, 7 days a week producing breathtaking music is no less intelligent, no less educated, and certainly no less hardworking than a super-high-earning CEO.

High earners can be categorized in six groups:

Group 1: inventors, businesspeople, designers, and people with specific talents. Because they are unique in their fields, they can reap huge amounts of money through sales, royalties, and the like. These talented risk-takers are rewarded accordingly but can lose big if the tide goes against them.

Group 2: CEOs who achieve their companies' short-term profit-maximizing goals using any means they can think of—such as outsourcing production, downsizing production facilities, laying off employees, and increasing sales—in order to increase the company's profit margin. For their performance, they garner huge bonuses and financial settlements. However, their actions have destroyed many people's lives economically, making it even harder to justify their compensation of 3,500 times the average income.

Group 3: Dishonest CEOs who falsify records, cheat investors and employees, and take a big chunk of their company's money for themselves and their associates. Enron executives and many others fall into this category.

Group 4: People who use tax money to open new businesses, including entrepreneurs who bring athletic teams to cities that agree to pay for a new stadium.[18]

Group 5: Scammers who defraud and cheat innocent people, financial institutions, and the government. Examples are subprime mortgage lenders and Medicare fraudsters.

Group 6: Brokerage firm staff involved in stock-market speculation and fraud, who enrich themselves at the expense of the majority of innocent, uneducated investors.

On further scrutiny, we can see that these six groups fall into two overarching categories:

• talented people whose large incomes are justified (although the question remains whether they need to earn several thousand times the average income)[19]

---

18   Johnston, David Cay: *Free Lunch,* Penguin Group (USA) Inc., New York, 2007.

19   It is preposterous that the elite capitalists use all their efforts to extract money from people through profit-maximizing drive, accumulate wealth at any price, and then turn around and give it back to the people after they have become poor! Elite capitalists give fancy names to this behavior, such as "creative capitalism" as propagated by Bill Gates, founder and chairman of Microsoft; or they may use more conventional terms, such as foundations, charities, churches, and the like. The economic and environmental damages and costs incurred by such actions far exceed any amount of money they later give away, even if they end up returning their entire accumulated wealth back to the people. Even if some elite capitalists have not been directly involved in wars, manipulations, speculations, subprime mortgages, or the other "bubbles" that have led to an economic downturn and financial

- shrewd businesspeople, speculators, manipulators, and scammers who should not be entitled to any compensation, much less the outrageous amount many of them get. To discourage or stop their activities, we need strong legislative action and severe penalties.

The real problem with income inequality is not so much that some people earn vastly more money than others and seems to enjoy better lives. It's that a culture of dishonesty and fraud develops that increasingly encourages shrewd people to use every possible tactic to enrich themselves. The associated social costs are staggering, as we have seen with the subprime mortgage fiasco, Medicare fraud, and stock market speculation (to name just a few examples). Obviously, income inequality creates unnecessary cost to the economy and is a major obstacle to realizing a zero-cost, carefree economy.

In the interest of creating a healthy, fair, zero-cost economy, we must not allow the incomes of a company's top earners to exceed 10 or 15 times the incomes of workers earning the lowest salaries in that company. This strategy has been implemented successfully in many U.S. companies, among them Costco. Although this approach can be debated, we must recognize that the smaller the disparity between these two groups' earnings, the greater the chance that the company will attract better and harder-working employees and achieve greater overall success (as with Costco).

The same approach could apply to a community, whether on a local, state, or national level, with the top earners' incomes not exceeding ten to fifteen times the lowest earners' incomes. Statisticians could create a method for calculating the average income for the highest and lowest earners at a given level

---

disaster for millions of people, they have certainly been a part of them indirectly. What an unnecessary waste of resources.

(local, state, or national). To come up with a sound method, we would need to consider every possible factor. For instance, a potential problem may arise if a company decides to distribute all its revenues as different types of benefits among employees while paying nothing to a local, state, or national fund established to help equalize incomes.[20] This would be a shortsighted decision, however, because these manipulations would be discovered eventually. In such a case, the company would have to pay into such a fund any amount that exceeds the local, state, or national average. This method would leave income tax in place.[21]

In a carefree economy, the government could use a method that divides a company's revenue into four parts, as follows:

---

20   This income-equalizing fund would use statistical data collected from all income groups. The data would determine the average annual income of the top earners (let's say $150,000) and bottom earners (let's say $10,000). A top earner making more than $150,000 would pay into the fund the difference between his or her income and $150,000. Conversely, a person earning less than $10,000 would receive from the fund the difference between his or her income and $10,000. Thus, someone earning $200,000 annually would pay $50,000 into the fund; someone making $8,000 would receive $2,000 from the fund. Welfare recipients would receive much less than the lowest earners, to encourage them to strive toward the next level. The best way to make this system function is for each state to create a separate fund, as the average income varies from one state to another.

21   The income-equalizing fund would have nothing to do with income tax, which is a federal issue. However, in a zero-cost economy, it's highly recommended that dividends received from investments in government-promoted projects *not* count as income. Also, as described earlier, this money should be exempt from federal taxes and should not be paid toward a state's income-equalizing fund if, by adding dividends to the income, it puts the total amount over the average amount for the state's top earners. In other words, dividends earned from these investments would be exempt from both federal taxes and state income-equalizing funds. This would create an enormous incentive for positive behavior and would help correct the income-maximizing drive.

- The first part of the revenue would go toward operational costs, including future reserves.

- The second part would be used for salaries and employee benefits, including those of the owners and CEOs.

- The third part would go to the government in the form of taxes.

- The fourth part would be used for shareholders' and investors' dividends. If there are no shareholders or investors, this amount would be divided equally among the first three groups.

The government could always use its share of revenues as incentive to drive companies to develop new technologies and products with certain specifications (as described earlier with regard to use of tax incentives). I do not mean to suggest that the government should be involved in decision-making for companies; instead, it should only provide guidelines and incentives. The rest is up to the companies.

This begs the question: Would income equality take away employees' incentives? No—in fact, it would help draw more talented people to a company and close the gap between the top and bottom earners. After all, a company's success does not depend solely on a few people, such as the entrepreneur, CEO, and other executives. Instead, it is based on the sum effort of all employees.

Some readers may wonder whether this approach might encourage some people not to work. In this regard, we must distinguish between employees and welfare recipients. Most employees would probably work hard to attain higher income levels. If a few lazy employees misused the system, they would face protests from colleagues or find themselves out of jobs and receiving the lowest income from the government in return for some kind of work. Some people might not want to work at all, preferring to live off welfare. In a carefree economy, they would be obligated to go to school for further education and mental improvement.

If we achieve the goal of reducing income inequality based on the plan described in this book (or a similar plan), we must create a fair taxation system that taxes the different income levels in the same manner. We cannot use a progressive system that imposes higher tax rates on those with higher incomes. Once income equality is implemented or has been achieved, everyone would pay a flat tax.

To implement this policy, we should exempt from federal income tax all individuals or families with incomes at the twentieth percentile or lower of the income scale. The remainder (those with incomes in the twenty-first through one-hundredth percentiles) should pay a flat tax of, say, 10%. The figures used here are examples only and may need some modification, but they convey my basic idea.

How should state tax revenue be addressed? This issue becomes more imminent when we consider that the state would need to generate more revenue to help achieve many of the projects described in this plan (such as free energy, free college education, affordable universal insurance covering life, health care, natural disasters, theft, and car insurance under one policy, and elimination of property taxes). To achieve its goals, the state must get its cut from the 10% to 20% of its top earners before the reduced income inequality goes into effect as described earlier. This approach should not cause outrage among the rich and superrich, for the reasons described throughout this book (especially in the several preceding pages) and in the interest of creating a zero-cost economy—specifically to achieve general economic security in a carefree economy and to reduce income inequality. Also, these groups would realize that they benefit from the free energy and other services described above, which they would receive in a much more secure economy and environment.

To emphasize, revenues derived from dividends invested in the government-promoted projects I have been describing, such as decentralized solar or wind energy systems, should be exempt from all taxes (federal, state, and local) for the period specified by the government. This rule should apply to companies, entrepreneurs, investors, and all other entities involved in these projects.

What about dividends from ventures other than the high-priority projects promoted by the government? These should be considered income and should be taxed as any other revenue according to the plan delineated above because the investors chose to invest in those projects to maximize their profits without serving the nation's economic interests. To repeat, the tax exemption would apply only to projects the government promotes. Good deeds in the interest of the nation's well-being must be rewarded heftily.

The vast majority of Americans aren't well-off enough to need to worry about wealth redistribution to begin with. How can people worry about it when the only wealth they have is in their home and that home is being foreclosed? What kind of wealth does one possess when one's entire livelihood is based on money borrowed at high interest rates? How many of us have several mansions in different parts of the United States or around the world to worry about? Far more of us are losing our homes to foreclosures. How many own anything that we can keep and that has considerable value? Even those of us who own houses or land are finding out that these provide no real economic security, given that we have to pay property taxes that may exceed our income. Nor does owning furniture, clothing, or jewelry bestow economic security, especially as we grow older. Economic security does not exist for younger persons, either. In fact, it is declining for them, as we have been seeing.

Another way in which the rich try to scare people about income equality and wealth redistribution is to label these ideas socialistic or communistic. One may argue about the validity of such claims. The concept of carefreeism is very far from socialism or communism. It puts us on the best path towards a zero-cost economy and a prosperous economic security. We may have much hard work ahead of us before we can achieve a zero-cost economy, but once we reach that goal, it will serve everyone in the best way. Fear of socialism and communism is totally misplaced. A carefree economy is the only type of economy that would create income equality on a fair basis. By promoting general economic security, it would reduce insecurity related to economic pressures and costs. In the process, carefreeism would discourage hoarding of money and the drive to accumulate extreme wealth.

Income equality is a goal worth pursuing, because striving for extreme wealth cannot guarantee better economic security or a better life if, in the process, it puts the striver at risk of losing everything in the stock market during a market crunch—or worse yet, lands him behind bars. We will not name the individuals who have served jail terms or the companies that went bankrupt in the past; nor will we predict which ones will face legal troubles from the 2008 Wall Street failures. The crimes they committed cannot be and will not be tolerated in the future; such greed and dishonesty must be punished harshly.

We might as well start thinking and acting the right way now and reducing income inequality is the most effective way to discourage greed and dishonesty. In fact, one of the beauties of a well-functioning zero-cost, carefree economy is that it would tremendously decrease the drive for greed and dishonesty.

Finally, the rhetoric some people use when discussing wealth redistribution requires some explanation. Most Americans get scared and paranoid when this topic is raised. But belonging to a political party does not make one rich. Likewise, social, religious, and political controversies have nothing to do with economic concerns. It's unrealistic to assume that the world's 7 billion inhabitants would agree on all social, religious, or political matters. However, they all have an interest in resolving economic problems and creating economic security. In my view, very few economic concepts are workable as the world's current economic woes suggest.

4) ECONOMIC IMPACT OF THE TWENTY PILLARS

The first step we must take is to implement a policy that delivers free energy to power the economy and optimize its functioning—from creating new jobs to providing free energy for vehicles and all kinds of buildings. Taking this initial step will lead us a long way toward reducing or eliminating energy costs which is a prerequisite to creating a zero-cost economy.

By providing free energy to power homes and vehicles, we can dramatically reduce or even eliminate energy costs. Savings derived from the use of free energy sources would bring substantial and permanent relief to private households. If a household's income stagnates, free energy can help compensate for that shortcoming. In this case, eliminating energy costs would have the same effect as increasing income.

Also, the relief gained from using free energy technologies would rid us of the financial burden of importing crude oil from foreign countries, thereby eliminating the need to keep U.S. dollars flowing to unfriendly countries, improving our staggering budget deficit, stabilizing our currency, and further reducing the costs of inland products.

The chain reaction triggered by developing alternative energy technologies can be far-reaching beyond our imagination. Possibly, entire books might be written about each positive reaction that occurs, whether economical, environmental, political, or related to national security. When you consider the compounding nature of increases in crude oil prices in the production process, the importance of shifting away from crude oil becomes even clearer.

By enforcing the use of decentralized solar energy technologies and conversion of gas-powered to electric-powered vehicles, we will create many new jobs in manufacturing and installation throughout Florida, stimulating our economy to an unknown dimension. And we could see these results immediately—as soon as the appropriate political decision is made. Practically overnight, we would be on the road to creating a dreamland.

These results are not possible if we rely on centralized energy delivery systems of any kind, including solar, wind, nuclear, or oil. Centralized energy plants do not create nearly as many new jobs as decentralized systems. At most, they create several thousand jobs compared to the hundreds of thousands created by decentralized systems. More importantly, centralized plants would not yield results for at least 10 years, whereas decentralized systems would deliver results virtually overnight.

Unlike decentralized energy systems, centralized plants are vulnerable to natural disasters. A natural disaster that struck a centralized power plant could render that plant inoperable for a long time—perhaps permanently. The economic cost would be anybody's guess. If a devastating hurricane struck a major energy plant, such as the Turkey Point nuclear plant in suburban Miami, all of south Florida could be pushed back to the Stone Age. But even if a natural disaster destroyed thousands of decentralized systems, hundreds of thousands of others would be up and running the next day, and the destroyed ones could be repaired or replaced almost overnight.

Using tax incentives, we should mandate that the manufacturers of more and more products such as cars, computers, and similar products sold in Florida (to be followed by other states) guarantee increased product lifespan and durability backed by a sound warranty. The German automaker BMW is not quite there yet but has taken the first positive step in this direction by covering all maintenance costs for BMW purchasers for the first 4 years or 50,000 miles; no other car manufacturer does that.

Furthermore, we should require modular design for these products to allow easier integration of product improvements and other updates. Companies that follow these rules should be awarded the "green" label, which would exempt them from the green tax and further enhance sales.

As these features of a zero-cost economy start to kick in and spread throughout the economy, replacement costs for these products would decrease (depending on the durability of the specific product). Product updates would not require product replacement, meaning consumers would not have to buy the latest version. By implementing this policy, we would reduce periodically recurring costs by at least 50%, assuming the product's lifespan would double.

Increased productivity in every aspect of the economy would further cut the cost of goods and services. Should productivity reach the ultimate speed, cost would decrease accordingly, drastically, and by greater amounts. In fact, productivity should be one of the most important goals of an economy.

Of course, the common perception is that productivity destroys jobs, which may be true for some sectors of the economy, assuming that demand is satisfied and has reached a saturation level. If increased productivity leads to saturation of demand, jobs would be eliminated accordingly. It's interesting to consider that if we could increase productivity to the point where all jobs were eliminated, we could manufacture products for practically zero labor costs. If we could increase productivity in every manufacturing sector, using robots to perform as much labor as possible, people in those sectors would never need to work in manufacturing and the products in question would be manufactured without human labor. Although this scenario is far in the future, we should not be surprised if it ultimately comes true, as advanced economies seek solutions from productivity. This development would indicate we have reached an ideal state and made great progress toward a zero-cost economy. The ultimate goal being a carefree economy, would bring us a leisurely and knowledge-based society.

Productivity is an area of economics that has yet to pique much interest, and it needs more serious research. Consider the Phillips curve, mentioned earlier. Its creator, Alban William Phillips, a New Zealand-born economist who did not have the foggiest idea how productivity might affect inflation when he developed his famous curve. Economics textbooks reflect this fact. Has anyone heard of the "speed" of productivity? Productivity is the ultimate tool for realizing a zero-cost economy. No economy can prosper without a permanent productivity increase.

By reducing healthcare costs, we can remove the major obstacle to provide healthcare for 3.2 million uninsured

Floridians and help provide higher-quality care. The measures described earlier can pave the way. Providing incentives to all participants, including service providers, patients, and insurance companies, can further reduce costs and increase the quality of service. Healthcare costs are the single highest social cost an economy bears—and they are unnecessary. We must do everything possible to reduce them. A healthcare system that is improved and reformed (from the standpoint of cost) will enable us all to live healthier lives and contribute more to a vibrant, cost-effective economy.

We must also protect the base of small businesses, which serve as the engine of the economy. As stated earlier, we must help businesses buy their buildings to decrease the cost of their products and services and help ensure their future existence. Rent is the one of the biggest costs for small businesses. By promoting building ownership, we can cut the cost of products and services and help businesses succeed.

Providing tax incentives to companies that manufacture environmentally safe, cost-free alternative energy sources would create new jobs throughout Florida, contributing to a booming economy and taking us closer to a zero-cost, carefree economy. It would also achieve another goal—giving the rich and superrich a way to make money without paying taxes. Keep in mind, though, that they would have to earn these tax savings through performance. We would not award them tax cuts simply because they are wealthy and might create new jobs in the future. In a carefree society, the rich and superrich will have to earn their money like the rest of us.

Taking control of extortionate interest and interest rates means defeating the biggest single source of cost for individuals, especially the poor and middle class. Companies that have borrowed money would benefit from controlling interest, as would all government agencies. Most importantly, saving money by reducing or eliminating interest would bring us a giant leap closer toward financing the cost of higher education and providing free education to all Floridians.

Enforcing the policy of home ownership described earlier would help resolve the social problems associated with homelessness, foreclosures, and real estate speculation—problems that are compounded by the drive to increase property taxes to unrealistic dimensions can cause communities to suffer boomerang effects. Furthermore, it is likely to minimize mortgage fraud, the stock market collapse, bankruptcies of financial institutions, and similar economic problems. To create a zero-cost economy, we must eliminate speculation of all types. We must create an atmosphere in which families have peace of mind and do not have to struggle to keep their homes. Freed from these threats, families would be in a much better position to engage in positive activities that could help prevent social costs of all kinds. In the long-run, everyone would benefit. A zero-cost economy would eliminate mortgage or rent for seniors. A paid-off house or lack of rent payments would benefit average families living on Social Security checks. Thus, home ownership is as important as free energy in achieving a zero-cost economy.

Free higher education for everyone is possible only in a zero-cost economy. The state could finance free graduate and postgraduate education by increasing the education fund in order to pay educators and cover overhead costs. Someone has to pay teachers' salaries and foot the bill for educational facilities. But if we use conventional methods without creating a zero-cost economy, it is just a matter of time before cost increases will reach their limit and educational costs will escalate again. Free education must be financed by the government, so we can build the future intelligent wealth of the economy. In a zero-cost economy, the cost of such financing will be relatively low and will not keep escalating and accelerating.

Encouraging ethical profit making, limiting lobbyists' influence, using specific tax incentives, and imposing the "green tax" and "health tax" will bring a drastic course correction to our economy, with the sole goal of creating a healthy economic climate that achieves overall cost reduction. While cost reduction is the ultimate goal of a zero-cost economy, ensuring a healthy, long-lasting, environmentally friendly economy is crucial, too. The measures described in this blueprint will help us achieve this objective.

The goal of a responsible government is to maintain households with surpluses that can be used as a reserve during lean years or hard times (for instance, those caused by natural disasters). Balancing the budget should be the immediate goal. A balanced budget indicates the state is financially sound and fosters confidence at every level of our economy and society.

To summarize, in the long run it's virtually impossible to build wealth entirely through speculation, even if some speculative activities initially bring substantial monetary gains. Similarly, people cannot build wealth if they have stagnating incomes and permanently dissipating purchasing power. They can build real wealth only when the cost of living for a person or household starts to decline relative to income. As cost drops, wealth can start to accumulate. If we can eliminate cost, practically all income can be saved, contributing to building true and stable wealth.

From a conceptual standpoint, this approach is possible if one starts to save all of one's income. In practical terms, though, people would not save all of their money. Inevitably, they would spend some of it on the goods and services they have always wanted. Yet in a zero-cost economy, many costs would be reduced or eliminated and would stay that way. Thus, in the long run, people would be able to build wealth even if they ended up spending (at least for the first few years) all the savings derived from cost reduction. Only in a carefree, zero-cost economy can a person build true, secured wealth. Reducing income inequality will enhance this process, making an ultimate zero-cost economy possible.

5) MAKING THE FEDERAL RESERVE BANK EFFECTIVE AND PURPOSEFUL

The Fed has two main jobs:

1) to employ discount policy by changing (increasing or decreasing) the interest rates, depending on the condition of the U.S. economy. By doing this, the Fed hopes to create price stability, full employment, and economic growth.

2) to supply money to the economy by printing it, or to withdraw money if the threat of inflation looms.

Unfortunately, these actions do not always achieve the desired goals, as I have noted throughout this book. The following example should clarify this point: Reducing interest rates, as the Fed did in 2008 during a period of conflicting economic conditions, did not have (and could not have had) the desired effect. It would be self-defeating to reduce interest rates to reduce unemployment while at the same time following a tight credit policy to avert the threat of inflation. Reducing the interest rate not only failed to accomplish the desired result; it had the opposite effect: It caused massive unemployment, forcing many businesses to shut down. Even worse, the low interest rate devalued the dollar on the international currency markets, worsening the U.S. terms of trade and making all imports (including crude oil) more expensive. Consequently, our economy started to take a dive. The need to follow a restrictive credit policy with regard to the real estate bubble was paramount to prevent further economic devastation that despite all efforts could not be prevented. The results were massive bankruptcy of giant financial institutions, a run on banks, and finally, a bailout of hundreds of billions of dollars.

So did the Fed accomplish its goals? No, it failed miserably. Therefore, we must ask, if the Fed is not and cannot be effective in using the discount policy to keep inflation and unemployment under control and create economic growth, what is its purpose? Its money printing-function does not justify its continued existence because the Treasury Department could do that at a much lower cost without incurring the expense of another huge organization.

To understand the gravity of this situation, realize that the Fed's shallow monetary policy would have led our country a long time ago to become a banana republic, if the U.S. dollar had lacked the status of a reserve currency among all nations because of our economic and military might. Since the Fed's policy keeps costing us no matter how we look at it, it is time we seriously looked for ways to make the Fed effective and follow policies that achieve that goal. Obviously, the Fed's conventional policy is deeply flawed. It's crucial that it switch to policies that make it effective and justify its further existence. However, when formulating a comprehensive solution, those responsible must think the entire concept through in the long term and from every aspect. And they should do so with the goal of creating an economy that effectively serves everyone—the poor, middle class, rich, and superrich—as befits as zero-cost economy. Although the Fed's ultimate goal is to maintain balance between the various economic factors, its overarching concern should be to preserve the nation's general economic well-being. If it achieved this goal, it would accomplish that task.

There are certainly more effective ways to achieve the Fed's goals of stimulating the economy and keeping inflation at bay. One way would be to supply and finance interest-free loans and mortgages to consumers—just the opposite of what the Fed has been doing. Reducing the prime rate, even to zero[22] (as the Fed was considering in the autumn of 2008), would not do the job. Consumers must be able to obtain zero-interest financing. This would work as follows:

1) The Fed would fulfill its usual position as head bank. Commercial banks would fulfill their usual function in executing the goals of the Fed whose policy is determined by the government.

2) The Fed would set different commission rates to compensate commercials banks for distributing loans and mortgages, instead of charging these banks the prime rate for borrowing money.

3) Loans for high-priority projects such as, decentralized solar energy systems would receive the highest commission rates—let's say 1% to 5% of the money borrowed for the period of the loan. The Fed would pay the commission to the bank and the borrower would receive this money at practically zero interest. The percentage the Fed would pay to commercial banks would cover the banks' costs in making the loans and collecting monthly payments. If a bank used its own funds, it would still get the specified percentage from the Fed at 1% to 2% higher than if

---

22 Guha, Krishna: Fed's dilemma over zero rate looms closer, in: *Financial Times,* October 30, 2008, P. 3; and, Aversa, Jeannine: Could Fed rate go to 0%? in: *Miami Herald,* FL October 30, 2008, P. 3C.

the Fed's monies were used. To emphasize, no money would carry interest when loaned to borrowers. The commission paid to banks would compensate them for making the transactions and handling the loans.

4) Loans for lower-priority projects would receive a lower percentage as compensation for the transaction, which again would be determined by the Fed.

5) Banks would follow the same strict terms to qualify borrowers for loans or mortgages. They should be held responsible for proper lending of their money as well as defaults on their loans and mortgages if borrowers fail to pay in a timely manner.

The following example will clarify this concept: Suppose the manufacturer of a decentralized solar energy system borrows money from a bank to manufacture the system. The bank lends the money at zero interest for a certain period—say, 5 years; the customer (manufacturer) makes payments without interest every month for the term of the loan. The bank gets its commission from the Fed until the loan is paid off. If the Fed decides to implement an expansive policy to promote a top-priority project, the commission percentage would be higher, enticing banks to make more loans in that direction. If the policy is to follow a contractive path, the commission percentage would be lower. This approach would be a substantial improvement over the Fed's current approach. One need not be clairvoyant to see its constructive and stabilizing effects.

It may take some time before the Fed, the economists, and the politicians start realizing the merits and effectiveness of the policy just described. Actually, the Fed seems to be wising up to the error of its ways by considering reducing the prime rate to zero. However, this move alone would not be enough to stimulate and create a strong economic foundation unless the Fed follows the other conditions of the policy I have delineated. The Fed, economists, and politicians must think through this and similar approaches painstakingly, and adjust policy accordingly. Until they do, no effective policy can be expected to stimulate and create a strong, healthy economy.

The effectiveness of the Fed's enormous Wall Street bailout during the financial crisis of September-October 2008 is dubious. If the Fed continues to bail out failed financial institutions and companies in the future, a series of devastating problems to the foundation of the U.S. economy will occur, leading to economic disaster. Bailing out failures is tantamount to joining failures. Bailouts are expensive, wasteful, and ineffective. In the end, they erode the public's funds and trust.

Similarly senseless is the Fed's current discount policy. Instead of bailing out failed financial institutions, the Fed should have used at least some of that money toward resolving the real estate foreclosure crisis, according to the policy advanced in this blueprint. Such action would have given hope to distressed homeowners and builders while providing an instant economic stimulus. In addition, the Fed would have projected a human face if it had reduced the length and level of monthly payments to make low-income housing affordable.

If my plan is followed, undoubtedly we will have many technical and other issues to address. Also, we should not expect a 100% clear-cut solution to our economic and financial problems. However, acting prudently and doing the right thing should take priority over everything else.

How much would my approach cost to implement? Much less, I believe, than the bailouts, recession, unemployment, foreclosures, loss of production, and other problems that have led to our current economic ills.

We must also ask: If Congress lets the Fed print money at will, why does the Fed lend money to commercial banks at the prime rate, with the banks in turn charging borrowers higher interest rates? Does no one at the Fed or elsewhere realize that this practice triggers the first round of cost escalation and acceleration, which compounds throughout the entire economy? If the Fed were to wise up and set the goal of reducing financing costs, it would see that its efforts to create full employment with stable prices could be achieved much faster and more effectively with the approach described in this plan than with its failed policy. It must be frustrating for the Fed to realize that it keeps repeating a failed policy! It is high time it looked at other solutions.

Combine the proposed commission policy of the Fed with the tax incentives described in this plan and the know-how to maximize productivity speed—and our economy would have three silver bullets in its economic arsenal to fight any type of economic woe effectively.

Chapter 5: ULTIMATE GOALS FOR DIFFERENT SECTORS OF THE ECONOMY

So far, I have explained the theoretical and conceptual basis of a zero-cost economy. Now I will describe how a zero-cost economy can be implemented politically.

Florida should immediately and effectively stop the economy from continuous bleeding and create jobs statewide, setting the stage for establishing a zero-cost economy. The ultimate goals are to provide:

- true home ownership for every poor and middle-class working family in Florida, making 100% ownership possible within 10 years

- free energy to power every house and vehicle in Florida

- a single insurance policy that covers all needs, including healthcare, life, automobile, natural disaster, and theft

- a banking and financing system based on (ideally) zero-interest operation

- an increasingly cost-free higher education

- advanced R & D and manufacturing facilities for renewable and environmentally friendly alternative energy technologies. These facilities would be the most advanced in the world, allowing Florida to lead the world in solar and wind energy technologies

- mandatory integration of active and passive solar systems in every new building.

Achieving these goals will require powerful economic and environmental policies, taking general interests into consideration. Some of these goals will necessitate the specific legislation, incentives, and deterrent measures described earlier.

1) ENERGY

This country cannot achieve total energy independence unless we rid ourselves of our dependence on energy costs or can gain access to free energy. From a financial standpoint, it makes virtually no difference whether we pay foreign countries for crude oil imports or get our energy from domestic facilities; in either case, cost will exist. (From a national-security standpoint, of course, we would be better off using domestic energy.) Furthermore, sources of alternative energy and the technologies involved in accessing them must be environmentally safe and immune from natural disasters.

Initially, we will need to take advantage of all energy sources to keep the economy going. But increasingly we will move toward generating energy from domestic sources available to everyone, such as solar and wind-derived energy. As we do so, we will create jobs all over Florida, not concentrated in a single location.

Fortunately, no country in the world is as blessed as the United States, and Florida is particularly fortunate. As discussed earlier, Florida will need to move overwhelming toward decentralized solar energy delivery systems and away from centralized systems (whether the latter are based on solar, wind, nuclear, coal, or any other source). Thus, the immediate energy plan should include:

- an aggressive policy for installing decentralized solar energy systems in every Florida home. This includes installation of wind towers as passive cooling systems. The state should pay for these systems in homes with market values below $500,000. For homes valued above $500,000, the state should offer interest-free financing and other tax incentives.

- conversion of gas- to electric-powered vehicles. The state should pay for the conversion of all existing vehicles operated by middle-class and low-income people.

- This energy plan would have far-reaching economic and environmental effects:

- It would create jobs statewide. For instance, in the manufacture of solar panels, tanks, electronics, photovoltaics, and the supplying enterprises, as well as in installation of these units by plumbers, roofers, electricians, architects, contractors and construction workers, etc. Other businesses would benefit from the booming economy when workers in the solar-power and related industries start to spend their income. The economy will boom in a healthy way, with abundant job creation and drastic, immediate lowering of energy costs.

- Converting gas- to electric-powered vehicles will have similar effects—creation of jobs state-wide, with thousands of facilities popping up virtually overnight to do the conversion work. Not only will this create jobs and provide free energy for transportation, it also will make working people more mobile so they can commute to and from work unhampered by exorbitant gas prices.

- Implementing the above two measures will have positive ripple effects, increasingly cutting the demand for crude oil and helping to halt America's economic bleeding by decreasing crude oil imports.

This energy plan represents a true stimulus package with long-lasting results. It would set the foundation for the next big project, described below.

Florida—the Solar Wonderland

The ultimate goal is to make Florida the most modern solar industry hotspot in the world, a true Solar Wonderland. Florida would become a more vibrant research and manufacturing destination than the denizens of Silicon Valley ever dreamt of. Solar Wonderland would become the world center for major research and manufacturing in every aspect of alternative energy (especially solar energy). The world would look to Solar Wonderland for answers to all future energy supplies.

Solar Wonderland would go far beyond developing sound technologies for powering cars and homes. It would explore possibilities for powering airplanes, ships, and spaceships and would set the stage for development of cutting-edge technologies that deliver electricity generated from Florida's sun to other states or that can be used to desalinize ocean water for domestic use. The future of solar energy development in Florida will know no limits, and opportunities for Florida's future in the fields of science and economy will be boundless.

2) TRANSPORTATION

Without ease of transportation, creating a zero-cost economy would be pointless. Thus, ease of transportation (especially free transportation) is a paramount goal, whether it involves public transportation services or personal vehicles. Communities that are more mobile are more likely to be ahead of immobile ones.

The short-term goal is to convert most existing vehicles to electric power, with solar energy serving as the primary energy source. We must promote free transportation powered by solar energy—if necessary, by exempting the sales tax on solar-powered vehicles. Although we have a long way to go before we will see reliable vehicles powered 100% by solar energy, we cannot wait too long; exorbitant gas prices soon may force some of us to stop driving altogether. Solar-powered vehicles may be somewhat limited in terms of speed and mileage, but in a zero-cost economy we would be able to operate them for free. The next step would be to use emerging technologies to improve the situation further.

3) HEALTH CARE

No healthcare policy can succeed in the long term unless it introduces cost-reducing factors, such as those outlined earlier. A sound healthcare policy must focus on:

- increasingly implementing preventive medicine to the point where virtually everyone is healthy

- improving productivity in healthcare delivery to reduce the cost of services drastically

- promoting health-inducing products, services, and activities, such as more healthy foods sold in restaurants and grocery stores, mandatory medical testing to monitor the development of everyone's health, and exercise and other health-related activities (such as spa services)

- reducing the need for curative medicine

- taking people off medically prescribed drugs as much as possible through enforced promotion of preventive and alternative medicine.

The ultimate goal is to create a society of healthy people with well-toned bodies. Unfortunately, the need for some curative medicine (such as for people injured by accidents) will always exist. Delivery of such medicine should be promoted through productivity-inducing facilities and technologies that offer first-class services at a relatively low cost.

If these measures are taken, we will see health insurance rates drop drastically. In fact, healthcare insurance will become an unnecessary luxury. 3.2 million Floridians will not need to worry about lacking insurance and others could save a great deal on insurance premiums.

4) HOUSING

To make home ownership as easy as possible and thereby strengthening the family's foundation and provide a secure place for families to live, Florida must eliminate the traps and pitfalls of the current housing market, which have had catastrophic consequences. We must take the following measures:

- Outlaw the Ponzi schemes used by some home builders. In these schemes, builders hype the housing market by selling the first few houses, condominiums, and other properties at lower prices to lure buyers, then increase the prices of the remaining homes arbitrarily. This forces buyers to speculate on everything they have so they can join the stream of profit maximizers. Although some of the people involved may reap short-term gains. In the end, this shortsighted practice hurts everybody—builders, buyers, financial institutions, and the state (in terms of property taxes).

- Outlaw subprime mortgages altogether, because they are the worst type of Ponzi scheme. Subprime schemes lead to fraud, robbery, dishonesty, greed, and stupidity, which devastate the finances of families, financial institutions, governments, and the overall economy. Even worse, they destroy Americans' trust in the economy.

- Limit mortgages to fixed-interest rates with the possibility of refinancing at a lower rate with no conditions or penalties attached. The long-term goal is to create a climate in which interest rates do not exist, which could happen if the Fed better understood the merit of this policy. What drives inflation is not the availability of "controlled" funds to finance the housing market, but related costs of all kinds stemming from fraud, schemes, and the like. Had interest rates not existed, the subprime scheme would not have been possible. Moreover, jobs are not created simply by the Fed's failed discount policy.

- Levy excessive taxes on properties purchased for speculation and business (rental) purposes, but exempt the first home of each family from this rule.

- Lower property taxes to an economically sound level until they can be eliminated or reduced drastically.

- Eliminate property taxes for families in which either head of household reaches age 65. For families owning more than one home, this exemption would apply only to one head of household.

- Stabilize home values, making them safe from speculation and property tax hikes.

If we took these steps, home ownership in Florida would be what it is supposed to be—the means to achieve a secure and sacred place for families to live and raise a better next generation. It should not be a source of despair and frustration for families.

5) EDUCATION

Free education from kindergarten through the university level is the most important service a government can provide its citizens. The government must supply the funds needed for this lofty effort.

To ensure a high-quality education, we must:

- Pay educators well so they can spend adequate time in class preparation, correcting homework, tutoring, and other essential tasks.

- Predicate teachers' pay on a base salary plus a premium determined by the quality of education they provide. The higher the grades a teacher's students score on state and local tests, the higher the teacher's premium. A formula to calculate the premium would take into account (among other things) the hours the teacher puts in, the number of students taught, and the teacher's effort in developing his or her own knowledge and teaching skills. We should further reward teachers who continue their education, to encourage them to continuously update their skills and expand their knowledge.

- Encourage successful people in all walks of life to speak from their experience, as a way to show their gratitude and give something back to society. We must encourage such civic services of all kinds.

- Ensure that students become more aware of the society they live in and show more respect to older people to create a gentler and more respectful society. We must avoid becoming a society of disengaged, demoralized, indifferent strangers. We must live like human beings, respect the elderly, value the family, and strengthen bond between families, our society, and the nation. Without strong family bonds, there is very little or no bond to society and the nation.

A society stands or falls on its citizens' education—or lack thereof. Education must take priority in every way.

6) EMPLOYMENT

In the future, employment will be less important. Currently, income derived from the family breadwinner's job no longer supports the family's livelihood; either this person must work more hours or more family members must work to cover permanently increasing costs.

With a zero-cost economy, we will need to work less and less as we move toward reducing and eventually eliminating cost. Therefore, the goal of our employment policy should be to implement measures to create a zero-cost economy, as explained earlier.

7) ENVIRONMENT

We simply cannot continue to treat the environment as we have been treating it. We must do everything possible to reverse the damage already done to our climate and environment or at least to prevent such damage from continuing and getting worse.

However, we have to live somehow, and every activity contributes to environmental decay, no matter what we do and how careful we are. The only way to make the economy compatible with the environment is to create a zero-cost economy.

8) BUSINESS

Business is the engine of the economy. For businesses to exist, they must make a profit. Yet the drive to maximize profits, as explained earlier, slows the economy by contributing heavily to cost escalation and acceleration. Runaway costs eventually lead to a permanent drop in purchasing power, which in turn results in an economic downturn. The results are unemployment, home foreclosures, deficits, inflation, bankruptcies, and finally sellouts of American companies and their properties to foreigners.

This trend must stop. We must revive healthy businesses and create more of them. We cannot contribute to the demise of more businesses even if they do not operate in the interests of the general economy. Whether we like it or not, many of these businesses provide the technologies we need to meet our economic goals related to energy and the environment.

Therefore, we must use every imaginable sound fiscal and monetary policy to channel these businesses in the right direction. Instead of maiming them with taxes, we should encourage them to help us achieve our general economic goals. Specifically, we must do the following:

- Encourage ethical profit making instead of profit-maximizing drive. This will enable companies to make a profit without sucking financial resources from our economy and citizens.

- Promote energy-saving and free energy-delivery technologies through tax incentives and direct payments to convert costly energy supply systems to free energy delivery technologies. This will eliminate a major cost for companies, reducing their operational expenses.

- Help businesses (especially small businesses) own their own properties. This will eliminate the need for them to pay rent—currently a major cost of businesses. Rent is subject to annual increases (whether justified or not) as well as property taxes that come out of the company's pocket (a preprogrammed cost-escalating factor). Building ownership not only would eliminate rental costs but also build equity for the business, which it can use as collateral against borrowed money if needed.

- Provide tax incentives to all businesses that develop high-priority technologies, such as solar and wind energies. Tax incentives should be extended to investors, along with the possibility of tax write-offs for those who invest in these projects. This is a fast-track policy and the best tax incentive for achieving any project the government can realize without advance investment (but with illusory taxes that never existed). It would give companies and investors major incentive to move forward by freeing them from all taxes on future investment income and dividends as well as on capital gains.

Future business activities will not resemble those we see today. Businesses will become more consumer oriented and less focused on maximizing profit. They will be able to make as much money as they want without engaging in destructive practices that emphasize short-term goals. They will have every reason to do all the right things and make all the profits they desire without imposing job layoffs or outsourcing jobs to other countries. In short, American corporations, especially those operating in Florida, will get more a human face.

9) PROPERTY TAXES

No responsible government (or anyone of sound mind) would increase property values, celebrate the bounties of increased property taxes, and then mourn the drastic decline in property tax revenues when property values start to tumble due to foreclosures and bankruptcies (even if the government can collect taxes through auctions). Celebrating short-term gains yet promoting activities that cause long-term losses is a bad policy. Even worse, few people seem to realize or care that a municipality's economic foundation can be shattered through the inept and imprudent policies that have led to a large exodus of families out of Florida.

To make Florida a dreamland, we have to make it economically attractive. One way to do this is to keep property taxes as low as possible so that living here is affordable for all. A municipality must have enough income to run needed services and day-to-day operations. But there are other effective ways to get this income, as outlined in this blueprint. Imposing property tax hikes on homeowners shows lack of intellectual capacity on the part of government officials. This mentality needs to change immediately.

No seasoned politician would base a budget on a temporary, short-term revenue increase. Such a shortsighted policy only entices officials to spend the increased revenues, create new job openings, and raise salaries. Then, when revenues start to shrink, the government is forced to downsize its workforce just to cover expenditures. This situation creates an endless chain-reaction of economic ills and financial suffering for the entire community.

Instead, wise and honest politicians should see themselves as a part of their community. This will encourage them to think long term and make economic and political decisions accordingly. The measures they enact should serve all citizens through old age, when people must depend on limited savings and the monthly "pity" income from Social Security. Unfortunately though, many politicians act in their own self-interest or their cronies' and contributors' interests.

In a zero-cost economy, people must be able to own their homes free and clear, especially before they reach age 60—somewhere between ages 40 and 60, but ideally long before age 60. No financial burdens of any kind, such as property taxes, should be levied on their homes. Thus, property taxes must be modest and not pegged to increased property values. Also, when any household member reaches age 60, the home should be exempt from property tax until the deaths of both spouses who own that house.

In a zero-cost economy, property taxes would decline and governments would need relatively lower annual revenues to operate facilities and provide services as they incorporate the principles of a zero-cost economy (assuming the number of households in that community remains unchanged). A rise in home ownership may call for more revenues. However, property taxes should be raised only as a last resort, after all other possibilities (such as cost-reducing measures) have been exhausted.

10) INTEREST

The ideal way to run an economy is to avoid interest entirely. One of the biggest cost-generating, cost-escalating, and cost-accelerating factors, interest also compounds at the same time. Unfortunately, eliminating interest is not possible now because interest is the foundation of the elite capitalistic economic system. Nonetheless, we must try to minimize its negative effects by keeping interest rates low. This should apply to every aspect of the economy, especially to financing alternative energy technologies and sources. The same should apply to families buying their first homes. In a zero-cost economy, interest will play a reduced role—and an economy with low or nonexistent interest is much better off.

11) INSURANCE

Like the Federal Reserve, insurance companies can sell and write policies—in effect, printing money at will (at least indirectly). This unique power must be made to serve the people. We must create a strong but efficient insurance industry that is aboveboard and works in the people's interest. Insurance companies should be required to cover policyholders with no exceptions or limitations when it comes to health care, natural disasters, and car insurance.

The first step toward correcting our current insurance problems is to drastically cut the cost of insurance-company operations, such as processing claims and premiums. Such cost-cutting measures would serve all participants. When a zero-cost economy is functioning to its full extent, insurance companies will replace their money-printing capability with a willingness to serve customers better at lower cost.

12) POVERTY

The goal of a zero-cost economy is to make people economically well off and create a true general capitalism. Some Americans blame poor people for being poor, claiming they got that way because they are lazy, unwilling to work, and prefer to live on charity and handouts. Although this may be true for some poor people, it does not hold true across the board. It is simply inconceivable that some people choose to be poor and live in misery.

Furthermore, as a great and fair society, we should not and cannot allow a group of citizens to suffer in poverty and other woes that go along with it. We must do much better. After all, rich people are the trustees of the poor. We must use all our efforts to improve the standard of living of the economically deprived. To do this, we need to distinguish between two groups of poor people—those who work hard but cannot make ends meet, and those who simply live on charity and handouts.

When we take a closer look at the causes of poverty, we see that lack of education, training, and availability of jobs loom large. The following measures will help the poor escape their poverty:

• We must educate the poor (especially those living in ghettos) so they can learn the necessary skills and knowledge to find work and thus earn an income.

• The skills they learn must be low-tech ones they can use in their own communities. To convert job training into jobs, we must create facilities in these communities. One way is to have impoverished ghetto inhabitants build prefabricated, energy-independent, hurricane-proof houses. These houses would then be sold to the workers who built them; financing would come from government sources and carry zero-interest rates, which would eliminate the need for all types of government subsidies for housing and other programs. To further improve employment in these communities, low-tech manufacturing plants (such as those that make solar water-heating panels) could be created. Instead of letting immigrants from other countries flood Florida, let's put our own people to work first.

• The next stage is to create stores and other businesses that serve poor communities, allowing them to generate income. This would create more jobs and income and help these economically deprived communities achieve a better standard of living.

My plan for reducing poverty is presented above in a nutshell. The complete plan is detailed and well thought out, based on my own experience.

13) VETERANS

A nation's greatness shows in how it treats those who have served it in times of need and crisis, especially those who have put their lives on the line to defend the nation or its interests. We cannot let our veterans rot once a war or other crisis ends. We must give them additional financial support, in terms of health care and otherwise—especially those who have suffered physical and mental disabilities. We must show our appreciation and compassion and encourage national pride. We can achieve this goal when we feel proud about who we are as a nation. No individual or nation can be proud when seeing its veterans living homeless under bridges. Life would become easier for veterans in a zero-cost economy, when better services can be provided at lower cost.

14) RETIREMENT

Old age brings many burdens. Older Americans should not have to worry about money. The golden years should be a time to enjoy one's remaining days on earth and prepare for the transition to the world beyond in a peaceful, dignified manner. The last thing seniors should have to worry about is where they will get their next meal or how they will be able to afford a place to live or a piece of land for their eternal resting place. The fact is, everybody grows old (except those who die young).

We must help make old age truly a golden time. Creating a zero-cost economy is the only way to do that.

Chapter 6: CONCLUSION

For America to remain the greatest nation in the world, we must reject our current ruinous economic and environmental policies and activities. We cannot continue to live on borrowed time and money or make devastating mistakes such as the one that saw us occupy Iraq in the hope of getting more oil (maybe safe and secure oil, and perhaps even free oil). As we have learned, the Iraq war has done nothing but cost us $551 billion (and still counting) and taken the lives of more than 4,200 American soldiers.

Let's engage in some serious thinking: Assume the Almighty God lifted every drop of crude oil in the world in the palms of His hands and relocated it to the United States, where we could use it cost free. Even if this scenario came true, we would not be able to use the oil for long because of global warming and its devastating consequences.

We need to drastically reduce our crude oil consumption so we can save it as the most precious source of raw material for our own and future generations. We must do everything possible to reduce our need for oil and eventually stop using it altogether, at least as an energy source, because of the global warming threat. If instead of spending billions on the Iraq war, we had spent it toward developing alternative energy sources, we could have generated enough energy to power the entire country and convert all the water of the Atlantic and

Pacific Oceans into steam. Sadly, we blew all of that money and wasted away all those precious lives and opportunities.

Because we cannot and should not rely on crude oil as our main energy source, we should start right now to do what must be done: Set the foundation for creating a zero-cost economy, which (when firmly established) would immediately start changing the economic equation in favor of a sound economy and a healthy environment. A zero-cost economy will create new jobs in abundance. Our dependency on crude oil will disappear slowly but surely, and within a few years we will be totally independent of it. The financial burden on Americans will start to decline, making our lives easier and less stressful. As we move increasingly toward a zero-cost economy, we will reach the ultimate goal—general economic security in a carefree economy.

Some readers may be wondering: Is creating a carefree, zero-cost economy the only way we can realize our economic and environmental goals? As we have seen, communism has failed miserably, socialism is taking the same course, and elite capitalism eventually will follow the same sad path. The most compelling reason to embrace the concept of a zero-cost economy is the all-important factor of cost. We cannot achieve a zero-cost economy overnight without implementing the concepts discussed here. We must cease our destructive behaviors immediately and keep an open mind about the changes that will be required. We can achieve carefreeism only through the concerted action of all Americans.

One of the most pressing questions is how to finance the measures described in this blueprint. There are many ways we can finance our primary goals of totally converting to solar energy and converting existing gas-powered vehicles to electric-powered ones throughout the entire state of Florida. Here are some of the ways:

- Divert some of the $20 billion available for "pork-barrel" projects toward jump-starting solar energy projects and converting gas-powered to electric-powered vehicles.

- Stop spending $30.3 billion on the Iraq war [23] and use that money instead on projects that would serve Florida and the nation economically, technologically, and from a national security standpoint.

Although this huge sum of money has been blown away, in the future we will need to be far more careful and concentrate on the most immediate and necessary projects—1) financing the expansion of solar energy and converting existing vehicles to electric power, and 2) providing free energy and transportation to all Floridians. If no other financing source is available, these two goals should take top priority as the first and most important steps toward creating general economic security in a zero-cost economy. Financing also could come from issuing state bonds, transferring money designated for "pork-barrel" projects, and diverting funds from economically less important projects.

Many other feasible financing options exist. For instance, we could create a state bank to finance the most urgent projects. In short, where there is a will, there will always be many ways. We must move forward toward achieving a zero-cost economy immediately and energetically. This time we should not and cannot lack the will.

It is not too late to invest in solar and wind technologies in Florida so that our state truly is the Sunshine State. We must not make the same mistake that got us into the Iraq war—

---

23   As of September 1, 2008, Florida's share of the cost of the Iraq war was $30.3 billion.

investing funds in the dying oil industry. This would only be another version of our failed Iraq policy. The era of dominance by crude oil is about to end. The beginning of the end will start in Florida.

What will become of the mighty oil industry once solar and wind energy begin to dominate? A responsible government would be wise to use all the technological resources of any industry, especially the oil industry and engage the oil companies in developing and manufacturing environmentally safe, renewable energy technologies and sources. To achieve this goal, we should offer generous tax incentives. The same should apply to the capital gains and dividends earned by investors in those companies. Any price would be worth paying, as long as these efforts help us create a zero-cost economy. Clearly, we do not want to fight the oil industry or any other sector of the energy industry such as coal or nuclear. Instead, we should use their resources and technological know-how to help attain a zero-cost economy. Accordingly, we should reward these companies fairly.

One last question remains: What about the recurring revenues that the capitalist economic system is accustomed to getting? As discussed earlier, a revenue for one person or business is a cost for another. The purpose of a zero-cost economy is to reduce, if not eliminate, all costs.

It would be naïve to assume that in a zero-cost economy, the source of income for the industries involved would dry up as more and more people became energy independent. The fact is, the world is unlimited. No corporation should worry about being unable to re-charge people for the energy if they get it for free. Corporations could sell energy systems to millions of homes in both this country and foreign countries. Their income sources will not dry up. Furthermore, the elite capitalists would be able to generate more income as the technology advances and they are once again in the position to sell or replace the old with the new.

Once energy is free, people will be able to save money and will be in a better position to purchase and replace old technology with the new. Elite capitalists will keep prospering as they sell energy systems that deliver energy for free. What's more, we will all experience a much better and more secure world and more rewarding lives. On the other hand, if the elite capitalists decide not to change course but simply continue their failed methods, eventually they will be haunted by the effects of their shortsightedness.

Realizing a zero-cost economy is the only way to provide a bright and prosperous future for Florida, both economically and environmentally. Let's all get involved and move forward quickly. Your future and your children's future depend on it.

EPILOGUE

I began this book in May 2008 and finished it in November 2008. It is available in three forms—a printed book, an e-book, and a free download available at www.zerocosteconomy.com.

The title for the printed book and e-book is *Towards A Zero-Cost Economy – A Blueprint to Create Economic Security in a Carefree Economy*. The title for the website download is *Towards A Zero-Cost Economy in Florida – A Blueprint to Create Economic Security in a Carefree Economy*. Although this book focuses on Florida, the economic policy it presents can be implemented by other states as well, with minor adjustments as needed depending on specific conditions in those states.

Regardless of how you access *Towards A Zero-Cost Economy*, we encourage you to visit our website often for updates and new articles—and simply to stay in touch with each other. We also invite you to submit your ideas, suggestions, and criticisms to the website so we can make these available to others. The zero-cost movement is not limited to any particular political, environmental, or religious group or ideology. It concerns and can benefit all of us—every human being on planet Earth. For the human race not just to survive but to enjoy general economic security and prosperity in carefree economies worldwide, the concept of carefreeism must grow and replace all the failed conventional economic concepts currently in use.

Of course, promoting a zero-cost economy entails more than just publishing a book on the topic and making it available on a website. Although, these are the first steps towards realizing that goal. Most important, we must all be involved, regardless of age, gender, race, political or religious views, or other issues that may divide one group from another. To create a grassroots movement, please urge your family members, friends, colleagues, and everyone else you know or meet to visit www. zerocosteconomy.com. For an even greater impact, ask those people, in turn, to urge *their* family, friends, and colleagues to visit the website ... and so on. Send them e-mails about the website, and refer www.zerocosteconomy.com to everyone you know, whether they live in the United States or a foreign country. For the zero-cost concept to prevail, the movement must become national and international. It must be adopted universally if we are to live in peace in an economically secure world. The power of the chain reaction you help trigger by spreading the word will move the zero-cost concept along and eventually help it to prevail and function on its own.

Creating a grass-roots movement in this way would reduce the tremendous costs involved in waging political campaigns. This in turn, would make it possible for other candidates—those with potentially better ideas but with less money—to run for office. Most importantly, it would force politicians to come up with new ideas, plans, and solutions rather than campaign on the polemics, rhetoric, and smear tactics we've become so accustomed to.

In the meantime, until the concept of carefreeism can stand on its own feet, I urge everyone to buy only American–made products. The United States is the only nation in a position to lead the world economy out of it current downturn and towards a zero-cost economy. But before we can reach this goal, we must put our own country back on track. Globalization, the North American Free Trade Agreement (NAFTA), and similar pacts have failed. In fact, they have caused economic and environmental problems that outweigh any long-term advantages they have brought. With their failed concepts, they belong to the past. We should never again follow policies or embrace concepts that achieve relatively small gains at the expense of long-term benefits for large numbers of working people. In the end, no country benefits from such policies and concepts economically or environmentally. We all suffer when shoddy products are manufactured in low-labor-cost countries for the sake of profit maximization and when these products are flooded all over the world with no regard for the limitations of natural resources and the environment.

Certainly, we need to trade with other countries for products we cannot manufacture or for our which manufacturing costs would be much higher. But the way we currently trade is a one-way street leading us on a fast track to poverty. We are exporting five times fewer cars than we are importing.

The United States consists of states that in some ways each resemble a country with some larger than Germany, Great Britain, or France and others as small as the Netherlands and Switzerland. Our states are so diverse that we may never need a product from another country, even if it is produced at lower cost. What we cannot achieve through low-cost labor we should compensate for by increasing productivity speed to the point where we can manufacture practically everything at almost zero cost. We must shun globalization if its main purpose is to maximize profit without long-term positive effects at least for the majority of the population of the participating countries.

Every American should be crystal clear on this point: Until we achieve energy independence, we cannot have any kind of security—whether economic, national security, or any other type—despite our huge military power and engagements. For the United States to become a truly independent nation and not have to worry about foreign threats or backlashes, we must put all our efforts toward becoming energy independent. To do this, we must develop all the energy technologies and sources that can provide free energy to all Americans to power our homes, buildings, factories, offices, vehicles, and transportation systems. As discussed and emphasized many times throughout this book, doing this will necessitate enforced development and promotion of decentralized solar and wind energy systems. In circumstances where we cannot use decentralized energy systems and must go with centralized energy plants instead, we should explore the possibility of providing very low-cost (preferably zero-cost) energy to users. By achieving this goal, we would be combating the biggest enemy of our economy—cost—and would enjoy a prospering economic security. Dependence on crude oil imports and low-labor-cost nations would be a thing of the past. Devaluation and flight of the U.S. dollar would be reduced to a minimum, if not eliminated altogether. The need to put our military troops in harm's way to protect our interests would decrease dramatically. Terrorism and religious radicalism would collapse of their own weight as the demand for crude oil dissipates. Finally, we could free our energy to looking toward a bright future for our nation and help other nations achieve the same goal.

At this time, our biggest concern is the confusion and sense of helplessness regarding how to jump-start and stimulate our economy. None of the ideas currently afloat contribute much toward achieving the goals that have been set. Their implementation would only deplete our resources and compound our problems further. Below I discuss some of the ideas now in vogue and reveal their fallacies:

- *Increase deficit spending on the infrastructure, as by building new highways, roads, and bridges.* Such spending would not create a significant number of new jobs. Unemployment is rising, and people who have lost their jobs cannot afford to put gas in their vehicles to drive on the new highways or bridges. Increased infrastructure spending might have value during the second or third stage of a stimulative, expansive policy, once the economy has been jump-started and is flourishing—but not until then. Certainly, we will need more new highways, roads, and bridges and the old ones will need to be repaired and expanded. Until we can boost the economy, we should concentrate first on the types of projects that can effectively jump-start the economy as described later in this epilogue. California has more freeways than all the European countries combined. Our first priority should be to reduce our dependence on oil imports while increasing Americans' purchasing power so we can afford to drive on our existing highways and bridges. We should not take the second step before we have taken the first.

- *Hire a significant number of new police officers.* This action would only compound our financial problems. Where would we get the money to pay for the new officers' salaries, insurance, pensions, vehicles, and gasoline? If our economic problems continue, no increase in the police force would be enough to protect wealthy off people from those trying to survive! Also, how would hiring more police officers help stimulate the economy?

- *Impose higher taxes on people with high incomes and corporations with high profits, with the goal of generating more revenue.* In this period of economic frustration, such a move would scare the stock market and plunge the economy further into a tailspin. Revenues derived from these sources would not be large enough to offset the costs

133

incurred by the reactions of individuals, corporations, and shareholders to the prospect of increased taxes.

- *Drill new oil wells.* This would lead to disaster when you consider how long it would take before we saw results as well as the environmental limitations and extreme costs. Drilling new wells would provide neither an immediate nor short-term solution; it would only lead to unnecessary costs at this critical time.

- *Implement projects such as centralized wind energy farms.* Farms such as those propagated by Texas billionaire T. Boone Pickens would not create a significant number of jobs anywhere. Should Pickens' plan succeed, it would achieve two things: slow the flow of U.S. dollars to oil-exporting countries and make him the richest person in the world. We should not fault him for his idea, which would put him above Bill Gates and Warren Buffet as the world's richest person. However, the average American would still keep paying for a permanently rising cost of electricity with no end in sight. On the other hand, if Mr. Pickens decided to concentrate on *decentralized* rather than centralized wind and solar energy systems, this approach would probably generate more income more quickly than his original plan—and would be greeted by great applause. He would become a true American hero.

- *Bail out distressed financial institutions and other distressed companies.* Although such actions are being seriously considered as solutions to a chronically flawed economic system, they are impractical. How long can the government continue to throw good money after bad before it hits the bottom of the pot?

It is high time for the government to come to its senses and take the right steps. Any action it takes must be effective, yield positive and immediate results, and entail the lowest possible implementation costs relative to those of other proposals. Any proposals put forward must achieve these five main goals:

- stop the financial bleeding by restructuring mortgages to reflect reduced property values and refinance at zero-interest rate

- stop massive unemployment immediately and rigorously, especially by bailing out the auto industry. (If we lost the auto industry, we'd lose far more than just an industry and would suffer more than just massive unemployment. America's mobility would become dependent.)

- create a considerable number of new jobs spread throughout the entire nation, in every state, city, and town—not just in clusters of several hundreds or several thousands here and there (as would be created by building centralized power plants, whether they produce solar, wind, nuclear, or any other energy or technology)

- increase purchasing power for a large number of Americans [24]

---

24 The Bank of Japan followed a zero-interest policy from March 2001 until July 2006 in an attempt to end the deflation that followed the bursting of Japan's bubble economy in the early 1990s. The purpose of the zero rates was to make borrowing money cheaper for consumers and companies to spend while making this money less attractive to save. However, this measure, sometimes called the "Japanization" of interest rates, would be insufficient to jump-start and stimulate our ailing U.S. economy and rouse it from its nosedive. The Fed must do much more. We need a drastic. rigorous expansion and immediate increase in purchasing power for both consumers and businesses. Besides implementing a sound, well-thought-out economic policy that extensively covers all critical aspects of the economy, the Fed must go below zero rates by paying commissions of 1% to 5% to commercial banks for handling loans and mortgages (a step we might dub the "Americanization" of interest rates). With this monetary policy, the chance of success would be much greater and the effects would be much faster and more far-reaching than with zero-rate experiments or any other variation. We simply do not have the time to experiment. For details of this policy, see Chapter 4, Part 5.

- have multiplicative effects throughout the economy.

The only feasible ways to meet these and other important goals immediately are to:

- enforce nationwide implementation of decentralized solar and wind energy systems

- convert existing gas-powered to electric-powered vehicles

- implement the plan I propose in part 5 of Chapter 4, which calls for the Fed to make zero-interest loans to consumers and distressed businesses and industries

- implement the federal and state tax incentives outlined in part 3 of Chapter 4 (the eighth pillar) as way to boost the economy. With job losses now occurring in record numbers, we must make every effort to avoid further loss. To achieve this goal, states should consider exempting American-made cars and products from state sales tax. The federal government and the Fed should compensate states as needed to make this policy possible and replace lost tax revenues. In other words, any efforts made must be aimed at increasing consumers' purchasing power on the one hand while making purchases cheaper and easier on the other.

Politicians and economists need to start implementing measures that primarily tackle the cost side of the equation, which would increase the gap between purchasing power and the cost of living in favor of purchasing power. Until this happens, no increase in employment or income generation will be enough to lift our economy from its steady nosedive, any results will be temporary. That's why it's so imperative for us to implement the economic and political measures discussed in this book. Piecemeal and inept measures that address problems incrementally will yield, at best, piecemeal solutions that are inept and incremental. We must be wise with the steps we take.

Finally, if we are to achieve impressive results, reducing income inequality must be an integral part of any short-term strategy and solution. For one, reducing inequality will discourage outrageous salaries, in turn causing the chief executive officers who seek such salaries to leave their jobs. For another, it will encourage people with greater talent to advance, contributing to a healthy, long-lasting, and vibrant economy.

A series of similar possibilities could also help stimulate the economy effectively and immediately, the blueprint provided in this book provides guidelines. Let us hope that far-sighted, judicious, and responsible policies and ideas will prevail and guide us during these challenging economic times.

APPENDICES

Appendix A: Comparing socialism and capitalism with carefreeism (zero-cost economy)

Issue	Socialism	Capitalism	Carefreeism
Employment	Employment figures include hidden unemployment; a minimum existence is guaranteed.	To maintain the same standard of living, people must work more hours; also, they are subject to losing their jobs and income.	Working hours will decrease once a desired standard of living is achieved. Hidden unemployment and lack of employment disappear.
Energy	Shortages occur; energy is cost-attached and its supply is unsecured.	Regulated through price and cost increases; always cost-attached; unsecured supplies; contributes to a decline in purchasing power.	FREE, abundant, and secured, contributing to increased purchasing power with stagnating incomes due to lack of cost.

Issue	Socialism	Capitalism	Carefreeism
Home ownership	State owns the majority of homes; private home ownership is not available to most people.	Most people supposedly own their homes, but attached costs (such as interest, property taxes, and long-term financing) make true ownership dubious.	True home ownership exists with no costs attached once the mortgage is paid off. Ownership is achieved more quickly and at a lower cost due to zero-interest financing.
Businesses	Most big businesses are owned fully or partly by the state to create jobs and employment for masses of people; small businesses are in a minority.	Most big businesses are controlled by elite capitalists whose primary goal is to maximize profits; small businesses create the majority of jobs and employment; profit-maximizing overwhelms and controls other goals and the economy overall.	Primary goal of any business is to help achieve a zero-cost (carefree) economy that serves the economic and environmental interests of the people and nation; ethical profit replaces profit maximizing.

ISSUE	SOCIALISM	CAPITALISM	CAREFREEISM
Insurance	Except for free nationalized healthcare insurance, other insurance must be paid for.	All insurance must be paid for; premiums keep rising to an unaffordable level.	Universal insurance policy at an affordable premium covers health care, car, life, natural disaster, theft, and flood.
Health care	Free but associated with a relatively low quality and long waiting times for specialized treatments.	Expensive; large segment of the population lacks any or adequate coverage; increasing costs make healthcare services unaffordable.	High-quality services are provided at relatively low cost due to manipulation of productivity, including technologies and efficient service delivery facilities. Preventive medicine, physical fitness, and proper nutrition are promoted

ISSUE	SOCIALISM	CAPITALISM	CAREFREEISM
Education	Practically free from kindergarten through the university level.	Free from kindergarten through high school; university-level education is very expensive.	Free from kindergarten through the university level. Graduation in multiple disciplines is encouraged through financial and job incentives.
Interest	Relatively low rates.	Rates change from low to very high, virtually reaching extortion level; subprime loans are permitted.	Rates, if any, are very low; ultimate goal is to eliminate interest altogether. Subprime loans are outlawed.
Taxes	Relatively high, to finance socialism and social services.	Relatively low, compared to socialist economies; however, elite capitalists promote arbitrary tax cuts for their own benefit; tax cuts have little if any benefit for the middle class.	Taxes cover cost of public services and promote business activities that serve the people and fulfill the nation's economic and environmental interests.

ISSUE	SOCIALISM	CAPITALISM	CAREFREEISM
Environment	Degrading; government makes little effort to halt the downward trend.	Economic interests and profit-maximizing drives overwhelm concerns over environmental degradation.	Economic goals are compatible with environmental conditions; one need not be sacrificed for another.
Natural resources	Devastated and exploited due to the need to provide for the population.	Devastated and exploited due to profit-maximizing drive.	Raw materials, such as crude oil and metals, are protected for future use; agricultural lands are enriched and improved to yield high-quality nutritional produce.
Poverty	Massive poverty exists, reflected in limited and low standard of living.	Tendency is toward massive poverty if increased cost of living isn't covered by income earned though increased work hours. Middle class tends to slip down to lower-income class.	No poverty exists; strong move toward creating a wealthy middle class.

ISSUE	SOCIALISM	CAPITALISM	CAREFREEISM
Retirement	At age 65 or younger.	Normally at age 65, but increasing to 70 and even older due to the need for more income to cover increasing living costs.	Everyone should be able to retire (from a financial standpoint) at age 50, unless they prefer to continue working for material gains or other goals.
Economic security and prosperity	Minimum standard of living is provided to all, but prosperity is available only to the political elite.	No economic security exists at all or at any given time, not even for the wealthiest. Prosperity is possible only as long as one works; increased prosperity requires harder and longer work or use of illegal methods such as fraud, plundering, and swindling.	General economic security and true prosperity exist, reflected by less need to work. (These are the main features of carefreeism.)

Issue	Socialism	Capitalism	Carefreeism
Society and the economy	Depressed society, with little incentive to improve one's standard of living. Sports, music, and art are the only areas in which to stand out or improve one's standard of living.	Plenty of incentive to improve standard of living exists, with no end to the struggle for economic gains and achievement of social status through material gains. Secure, lasting prosperity is practically an unreachable dream for most people.	Material gains are reached relatively early in life, leaving plenty of time and resources (one's own savings and wealth) to enjoy a leisure and knowledge-based-society.

Issue	Socialism	Capitalism	Carefreeism
Unethical methods of enrichment	Large-scale unethical operations are available only to the political elites; most other citizens can engage only in petty stealing and fraud.	Entire economy is based on the drive for fast enrichment, using such unethical methods as profit maximizing, late-fee charges, and high interest rates; fraud, plundering, swindling, and other schemes are commonplace.	Possibilities for unethical enrichment are few and discouraged (although a few people will find ways to cheat the system). Implementation of income equality and ethical profit making are cornerstones for decreasing the use of unethical means of enrichment.
Purchasing power	Declines permanently; must be compensated for with salary increases.	Declines permanently and must be boosted through increased salary or other methods, such as fraud, swindling, and plundering.	Purchasing power improves through income increases and reductions in overall costs.

ISSUE	SOCIALISM	CAPITALISM	CAREFREEISM
Currency	Tendency to become devalued.	Devaluation occurs against some currencies and revaluation against others.	Currency is always strong and revaluing, unless exposed to currency from a better-run zero-cost economy.
Income equality	Great discrepancy exists between high and low income earners, with no attempts made to reduce it.	Extreme discrepancy exists between high- and low-income earners, with middle class disappearing as some become elite capitalists and others join the ranks of the poor. No serious attempts, other than handouts in the form of tax credits, are made to reduce income inequality, but these attempts are ineffective.	Main goal is to eliminate *extreme* poverty and wealth; income equality does not mean equalizing all incomes. Reducing income inequality furthers discourage fraud, swindling, and plundering.

Issue	Socialism	Capitalism	Carefreeism
Productivity	Altogether ignored as an economic factor.	Not properly or extensively researched or implemented.	One of the main pillars of a zero-cost economy. Ultimate speed of productivity must be implemented in every area of industry and the economy to cut costs and increase purchasing power.
Economic growth	Falsified and distorted through social costs; no indications exist for economic gains of any kind; represents a major shortcoming for measuring economic progress.	Falsified and distorted through social costs; no indications exist for economic gains of any kind; represents a major shortcoming for measuring economic progress.	Tangible and measurable with the introduction of Economic Security Indices. (See book for details.)

ISSUE	SOCIALISM	CAPITALISM	CAREFREEISM
Inflation	Reflected in low-quality good and services.	Tendency toward inflation occurs unless controlled by increased productivity; inflation is preprogrammed into the system.	Possibility of inflation is minimized if not eliminated, as the system is designed to eliminate costs of all types.
Deflation	Chronic; goods and capital are scarce.	Exists during recession and depression; people and businesses fall victim to bankruptcies and total loss; money and capital are inadequate for manufacturing and job creation, while income is insufficient for people to purchase manufactured goods.	Exists during recession and depression; people and businesses fall victim to bankruptcies and total loss; money and capital are inadequate for manufacturing and job creation, while income is insufficient for people to purchase manufactured goods.

ISSUE	SOCIALISM	CAPITALISM	CAREFREEISM
Economic booms	Possible, but a socialist planned economy doesn't always lead to booms.	Result from deficit spending, subprime loans, and economic bubbles; once their effects disappear or the bubble bursts, recession and depression follow.	Healthy, booming economy exists without busts or rollercoaster effect, opening new economic horizons and dimensions.
Economic recession and depression	Chronic recession	Recession or depression is guaranteed after any economic boom.	Lack of sporadic economic booms means no recession or depression occurs.

Appendix B: Goals of carefreeism

ISSUE	IMMEDIATE GOALS OF CAREFREEISM	ULTIMATE GOALS OF CAREFREEISM
Employment	Full employment will occur within 1 year, achieved mainly through enforced implementation of decentralized energy systems. Passive cooling systems, conversion of existing vehicles from gas-powered to electric in manufacturing and installation will be rigorously promoted. Construction of productivity- inducing healthcare clinics is promoted to increase the number of construction jobs.	Create the conditions that will make retirement possible after age 50 and allow the transition from working life toward a leisure and knowledge-based society.

Issue	Immediate goals of carefreeism	Ultimate goals of carefreeism
Energy	Decentralized energy systems (solar, wind, and passive) will be promoted, which will drastically reduce energy costs. Research, manufacturing, and installation of these systems also will be strongly promoted. FREE energy will be provided to power Florida homes, buildings, offices, factories, and motor vehicles and other means of transport.	Florida will become a "Solar Wonderland," making it the world leader in research, development, and manufacturing.
Home ownership	Home ownership will be possible for every Florida family within 15 years at a maximum interest rate of 3%.	Every Florida family could own a home within 10 years; mortgage will be at zero interest rate.
Insurance	All Floridians will receive AFFORABLE, HIGH-QUALITY healthcare coverage.	Universal insurance policy will cover health care, car, life, natural disaster, theft, and flood at an affordable premium.
Health care	Alternative and preventive medicine, physical fitness, and proper nutrition will be promoted.	Population will become healthy, with well-shaped bodies and increased life span.

Issue	Immediate goals of Carefreeism	Ultimate goals of Carefreeism
Small businesses	Each business will own its building through zero-interest financing and other incentives.	Each business will own it building through zero-interest financing and other incentives.
Large, small, and new corporations	Businesses will get long-term tax exemptions for developing and manufacturing preferred projects that serve the general economic and environment interests of the state and nation; the same exemptions will be extended to all investors. Investors will be able to write off investments and receive tax exemptions on capital gains and dividends.	Same as immediate goals, until a leisure- and knowledge-based society is achieved. Tax exemptions will continue for projects that serve the general economic and environment interests of the state and nation.
Education	Free (including graduate and post-graduate education). All hardworking educators will receive financial and other incentives; high-performing and outstanding educators of all types will have guaranteed jobs and income.	Free, with financial incentives for students graduating in multiple disciplines, whether from a higher university education, professional training, or a combination of the two.

Issue	Immediate goals of carefreeism	Ultimate goals of carefreeism
Interest	Interest rates will be reduced so they don't exceed 3% annually for home financing; subprime loans will be outlawed. No interest rate will exceed 5% for any kind of financing, loans, credit cards, etc.	Interest rates will be eliminated altogether for home financing, energy systems, and electric- powered vehicles.
Property taxes	Will drop drastically; homeowners older than age 50 will not have to pay property taxes.	Eliminated totally
General economic security for everyone	<u>Step 1:</u> Living costs will be frozen. <u>Step 2:</u> Living costs will be reduced. <u>Step 3:</u> Living costs will be eliminated to the extent possible; purchasing power will increase steadily (as described in book).	Carefree economy will exist, allowing true ownership and sufficient savings and wealth (which will make possible a higher standard of living and improved quality of life) until the demise of two seniors (wife and husband) in households with existing accumulated savings and wealth.
Retirement	At age 60 from working life	At age 50 from working life
Veterans	Will receive free health care and easy home ownership	Will enjoy zero-cost living

ISSUE	IMMEDIATE GOALS OF CAREFREEISM	ULTIMATE GOALS OF CAREFREEISM
Poverty	Jobs will be created in manufacture of prefabricated, energy-free, hurricane-safe housing as well as in low-tech solar manufacturing facilities in low-income and depressed areas. These houses will be sold (at easy terms) first to people living in these areas, and then to those in other locations, creating a self-sustaining economy. Solar panels will be sold statewide.	Facilities will be created to accommodate increasing income in areas where the economy starts to take off, such as shopping malls, restaurants, spas, and clinics.
Environment	Will be restored to a safe, clean, and healthy condition.	Will be restored to a safe, clean, and healthy condition.
Natural resources	Agricultural land will be protected from nutrient depletion to increase its nutritional value. Use of alternative energy technologies to replace crude oil will be enforced. Recycling will be enforced.	Same as immediate goals, plus improved efficiency and productivity in implementing and realizing these goals.

Issue	Immediate goals of carefreeism	Ultimate goals of carefreeism
Income	General purchasing power will increase.	Income inequality will be decreased to retard speculation, exploitation, greed, plundering, swindling, and manipulation.
Purchasing power	Purchasing power will be increased by freezing, reducing, and eliminating costs of all types and by increasing income. (*Note:* No income can increase purchasing power unless income grows faster and forever; otherwise, costs will catch up with and exceed income; purchasing power is reduced according to rising costs.)	True savings and wealth will accumulate as a healthy, safe economy free of greed, speculation, exploitation, plundering, swindling, and manipulation is created.

Issue	Immediate goals of carefreeism	Ultimate goals of carefreeism
Society and economy	General capitalism will be created by increasing the wealthy middle class; elite capitalism will exist in a healthy, safe economic and social environment.	Leisure- and knowledge-based economy and society will be created in which people can move toward greater dimensions of knowledge and beyond the primitive economic world we now live in (which is controlled by greed, speculation, exploitation, plundering, swindling, manipulation, and war).

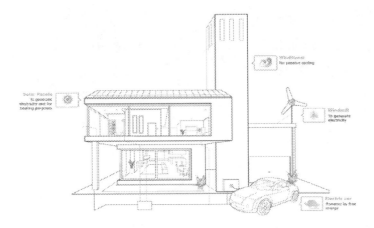

A typical **Zero-Cost Economy house**, powered by a decentralized energy system. A house with **free energy supply** is the foundation for the realization of a Zero-Cost Economy.

To jump-start the economy in a sound, healthy direction - with the ultimate goal of creating general economic security in a carefree economy - the purchasing power of the masses must be increased by means of reducing and eventually eliminating living costs. This goal can be achieved only through enforced development and installation of the decentralized energy systems described in this book and shown in this picture. Under the present economic conditions, no other measure can be as effective.

BIBLIOGRAPHY

Aversa, Jeannine: Could Fed rate go to 0%? in: *Miami Herald,* October 30, 2008.

Brant, Bob. *Build your own electric vehicle.* McGraw-Hill/TAB Books, New York, 1994.

Giles, Jim. Born to be wired. Stunning performance, awesome economy, no compromise. *New Scientist,* September 20, 2008.

Guha, Krishna: Fed's dilemma over zero rate looms closer, in: *Financial Times,* London, England, October 30, 2008.

Johnston, David Cay: *Free Lunch.* Penguin Group (USA) Inc., New York, 2007.

Kellard, Joseph. Don't narrow my gap! Why narrowing "income gaps" is unjust. *Capitalism Magazine,* February 28, 2004.

Khavari, Farid A. *Carefreeism—Economic Security in a Carefree Economy* (to be published mid-2009).

Khavari, Farid A. *Environomics—The economics of environmentally safe prosperity.* Praeger, Westport, CT and London, 1993.

Khavari, Farid A. Prerequisites for an efficient substitution of crude oil, in: *Ekonomska Analiza,* Belgrade, Yugoslavia, 1976.

Khavari, Farid A. *Vultures - Doctors, Lawyers, Hospitals and the Insurance Companies, What's Wrong, and What to Do About It.* Roundtable Pub., 1991.

Krugman, Paul. Faltering meritocracy in America. *The Economist,* London. January 1, 2005.

Leonardt, David. Time to slay the inequality myth? Not so fast. *New York Times,* January 25, 2004.

Machan, Tibor R. (ed.). *Liberty and Equality.* Hoover Institution Press, 2002.

Milne, Richard. U.S. becomes the low-cost site of the moment for manufacturers. *Financial Times,* London, England, September 8, 2008.

Pizzigati, Sam. The rich and the rest. *The Futurist,* July/August 2005.

Rector, Robert and Hederman, Jr., Rea S. Two Americas: One rich, one poor? Understanding income inequality in the United States. Heritage Foundation, August 8, 2004.

Walberg, Herbert and Bast, Joseph L. (eds.). *Education and Capitalism: How Overcoming Our Fear of Markets and Economics Can Improve America's Schools.* Hoover Institution Press, 2003.

Walker, Matt. Superfoods wanted. *New Scientist,* London, September 13, 2008.

Waters, Richard and Harvey, Fiona: Squeeze is on as interest grows in solar sector, in: *Financial Times,* London, England, June 2, 2008.